Vagabonds

Vagabonds

Lorae Parry

Victoria University Press

VICTORIA UNIVERSITY PRESS
Victoria University of Wellington
PO Box 600, Wellington

in association with
THE WOMEN'S PLAY PRESS
PO Box 9318, Te Aro, Wellington

© Lorae Parry 2002

ISBN 0 86473 435 2

First published 2002

Permission to perform these plays must be obtained from Playmarket,
PO Box 9767, Courtenay Place, Wellington, New Zealand. The
publishers acknowledge the assistance and advice of Playmarket, which
was established in 1973 to provide services for New Zealand playwrights

National Library of New Zealand Cataloguing-in-Publication Data
Parry, Lorae.
Vagabonds / Lorae Parry.
(New Zealand playscripts)
ISBN 0-86473-435-2
1. Actors—New Zealand—Drama. 2. Traveling theater—
New Zealand—Drama. I. Title. II. Series.
NZ822.2—dc 21

Published with the assistance of
a grant from

Printed by Astra Print, Wellington

First Performance

Vagabonds was first performed at Downstage Theatre, Wellington, on 13 October 2000, with the following cast:

CHARLOTTE BADGER	Lorae Parry
KATHRYN HORTON	Stephanie Wilkin
ADELAIDE FOLEY	Sylvia Rands
CAMERON CARRUTHERS	Steven Ray
RICHARD SWAN	Peter Daubé
SHIP'S CAPTAIN, WALLY, CAPTAIN PETERS	John Wraight
LUCY, MASKED AUDIENCE MEMBER	Phylli JasonSmith
BEN KELLY, PORTER	Louis Sutherland
CATH HAGERTY	Gareth Farr
MASKED SAILORS & MASKED CORPORALS	Cheryl Hoskins Antoon Moonen John Nayagam

Director	Annie Ruth
Composer and Musical Director	Gareth Farr
Set Designer	Nicole Cosgrove
Lighting Designer	Lisa Maule
Costume Designer	Janet Dunn
Stage and Production Manager	Cerridwyn Young
Production Assistant	Jocelyn Francis
Assistant Stage Manager	Moira Aberdeen
Fight Choreographer	K.C. Kelly
Lighting Operator	Jo Kilgour
Publicists	Pauline Harper Allie Webber

Acknowledgements

Special thanks to Gill Greer, Professor Vincent O'Sullivan, Dale Ferris, Playmarket, and to all the members of the original cast; Annie Ruth and Gareth Farr for their inspiration and vision.

I wrote *Vagabonds* during my tenure as writer in residence at Victoria University of Wellington in 1998. It involved a substantial amount of research into New Zealand's pioneer past: the arrival of the first performers in the early 1800s, the Land Wars and the life and times of New Zealand's first recorded Pakeha woman. Having the residency gave me the gift of the time I needed to write the largest scale piece I have attempted to date.

Playwright's Note

In writing the play, I was interested in exploring some aspects of New Zealand's past. I wanted to reach back as far as I could to our theatrical and Pakeha origins. As a result the play touches on the lives of some of the first professional theatrical performers who came to this country, and the first recorded Pakeha woman.

The play is set against the backdrop of the Waikato Wars. Three of the characters in the play are inspired by real people: Mrs Foley, Mr George Swan, and Charlotte Badger. I have tried to capture the essence of their characters by drawing from as many known facts as possible. Beyond that I have fictionalised wildly.

Mrs Foley was an actress and singer. She was the most celebrated professional actress last century. By the 1850s she was virtually a household name throughout New Zealand. She left her equally famous husband, Mr Foley, (who ran Foley's Circus) and began her own theatre company. She was a woman of many talents who had a penchant for young leading men. She had numerous affairs, and was renowned for having broken many a heart. Mrs Foley and her troupe performed in theatres and barracks throughout the country, and were a favourite with the garrison.

Mr Swan was one of New Zealand's first professional photographers and well reputed as an amateur actor. He had a thriving photographic business on what is now Stuart Dawson's corner. Many of the early photographs of Wellington were taken by Mr Swan. He toured and performed with Mrs Foley and became her lover until she eventually left him for another leading man. Mr Swan later became the Mayor of Napier.

Charlotte Badger was New Zealand's first recorded European woman. While she arrived in 1806, I have played with time and placed her fifty years later, in the same way as I have deliberately used anachronisms to link the past to the present. Charlotte was a colourful character with a colourful past, a convict who was transported from England to the rigorous penal colonies of New South Wales. While being taken to Tasmania on a passenger ship,

she and fellow convict, Cath Hagerty, teamed up with the first
mate, Ben Kelly, and between them they incited the ship's crew to
mutiny. Diverting the boat to New Zealand, they landed in the
Bay of Islands, where Charlotte is said to have lived for a time
with her small daughter, amongst Maori. Reports have it that on
the trip across the Tasman, she whipped the captain and donned
his clothes. I have used this as a springboard to play with cross-
dressing and gender, which, together with Mrs Foley's theatricals,
led me to Shakespeare.

Finally I was interested in the notion that when the European
colonials came to New Zealand they treated it as a new country,
forgetting that New Zealand was already 'an antique land'.

This play does not purport to be a factual record of real events or
real people. For purposes of dramatisation, characters have been
created, names have been changed and incidents have been devised
or altered.

Kathryn learns her lines. *Photo by Celia Warmsley*

Cameron and Richard—'And you, my dear chappy, are a poor excuse for a paramour.' *Photo by Celia Warmsley*

Above: Richard and Adelaide—'Do I make you nervous, Mr Swan?' *Photo by Celia Warmsley*

Below: Charlotte and Kathryn—'You stole an entire ship! You're not entirely innocent!' *Photo by Celia Warmsley*

Charlotte and Kathryn—'Make me a willow cabin at your gate . . .'
Photo by Celia Warmsley

Characters

The play begins aboard a ship in the Tasman Sea in 1853 and continues in Wellington and Auckland in July 1863. The play can be performed with a cast of twelve or more actors, but for professional purposes it can be performed with a cast of six adult actors, a ten-year-old child and an optional musician.

CHARLOTTE BADGER	A female convict, from Worcestershire, England
KATHRYN HORTON	An English actress in her late 30s
ADELAIDE FOLEY	An English actress in her 50s
CAMERON CARRUTHERS	An English actor in his 40s—Kathryn's fiancé
RICHARD SWAN	A young professional photographer and amateur actor
Various Characters (Played by one actor)	PORTER WALLY CAPTAIN PETERS
LUCY (Child)	CHARLOTTE's ten-year-old daughter

Other Characters:

CAPTAIN	Captain of ship, played by actor who plays CAMERON
BEN KELLY	The first mate, played by actor who plays RICHARD
CATH HAGERTY	Female convict, played by the actor who plays KATHRYN
MASKED CORPORALS	Played by the actors who play RICHARD and ADELAIDE
MASKED AUDIENCE MEMBER	Played by the actor who plays CAMERON
MASKED SAILORS	Played by the actors who play KATHRYN and CAMERON

'I met a traveller from an antique land . . .'
—Shelley

Prologue

Operatic music is heard. Mrs Adelaide Foley—*an imposing English actress, in her mid-50s, is standing centre stage. She is singing (miming) a piece of opera. She wears an exquisite gown and is beautifully lit. As she 'sings', she moves her arms in fluid, slow motion. They are outstretched, cajoling, seducing, imploring her* 'Audience'. *The effect is surreal.*

In tableau, at the back of the stage, are three people: Charlotte—*a convict woman, is in the middle. On one side of her, is* Cath Hagerty—*a female convict, and on the other side is* Ben Kelly—*the first mate of the passenger ship* Venus. *The two women are dressed in worn rags.* Ben *has one hand on* Charlotte*'s breast and the other hand up her skirt.* Cath Hagerty *has her mouth pressed to* Charlotte*'s.*

At the front of the stage are three people, two adults and a child, holding half masks—they are the 'Audience'. *They sit in the box seats of an elegant London theatre, in the mid 1800s. As the lights fade, the small* 'Audience' *claps.* Adelaide *and the* 'Audience' *fade off, as the three characters in the background come to life.* Charlotte *kisses* Cath Hagerty *and then* Ben. *They are obviously a little drunk.*

Scene 1: Aboard Ship—Tasman Sea, 1853

Charlotte, Ben Kelly *and* Cath Hagerty *are aboard the* Venus, *off the Tasmanian coast.* Charlotte *is being kissed and fondled by her two companions. There is a baby wrapped in dirty rags lying on a wooden pallet. When they come up for air, they hand a rum flask between them. They resume their lusty pursuits and talk in between kisses and caresses.*

15

BEN: You got a beautiful teet, Charlotte.
CHARLOTTE: I 'ave Ben, an' it's yours to milk, if you tug it right.
BEN: That's a decent handful, that is. What say we hit the deck ladies?
CATH HAGERTY: Wot say the captain comes in?
CHARLOTTE: I think we should turn this tank around, Ben!
BEN: Your wish is my command, Charly darly.
CATH HAGERTY: Play it right and you can grab the helm, Benny.
CHARLOTTE: Play me right, you can grab *my* helm, Benny.
BEN: Ooh, ladies, now you're exciting me to mutinous proportions.
CATH HAGERTY: He don't need much convincin', do he?
BEN: You're right there, darlin'.
CHARLOTTE: What say we toss the captain overboard, Ben?
BEN: Whatever you say, Charly . . .

> BEN *gets back to the task at hand, kneeling down and kissing and fondling* CHARLOTTE.

CHARLOTTE: Give him a short little ride in a longboat.

> BEN *puts his hand up* CHARLOTTE'*s skirt.*

CATH HAGERTY: Or a long little ride in a short boat.
CHARLOTTE: How does that grab ya, Ben?
BEN: Ooh, that grabs me . . .

> CATH HAGERTY *and* CHARLOTTE *kiss each other and* CATH HAGERTY *takes over fondling the breast that* BEN *now neglects.*

BEN: That grabs me very nicely . . .
CHARLOTTE: I say we screw Van Diemen's Land.
BEN: It's gotta be screwed . . . It's a pig of a place.
CHARLOTTE: That's right, Ben. Course we don't wanna dock here, do we?
BEN: Course we don't.
CATH HAGERTY: You sail her somewhere else, Ben.
BEN: Just name the place, ladies! The ocean is our oyster. Where'll it be then? Samoa, Rarotonga, New Zealand. Now that's a nice little port, ladies. Plenty of sun, sea, sexy little native titties.
CATH HAGERTY: Anywhere's better than this filthy hell!
BEN: Course it is. Bay of Islands will it be then?

CHARLOTTE: That's good, Ben. Cause you know how to drive this tub, don't you? You know how to turn 'er round, don't you?
BEN: I'm a dab hand at the wheel, ladies.
CATH HAGERTY: You'd make a good captain, Ben!
BEN: You leave the steering to me, ladies . . .
CHARLOTTE: An' you leave the navigating to me.
BEN: You run a tight ship, Charly . . .
CHARLOTTE: That's right, Ben.

> CHARLOTTE *directs* BEN'*s hand which is well and truly lost beneath the folds of her skirt.*

CHARLOTTE: Ooh, little to the left, Ben . . . that's right . . . up a bit . . . down a bit . . . that's good . . . that's good . . . Wot say we truss him up tonight?
BEN: Truss who up?
CHARLOTTE: The captain. Wot say we truss the captain up.
BEN: Ooh that's a juicy piece of pussy, Charly.
CHARLOTTE: Tie him to the mast, Ben!
CATH HAGERTY: Aye! Take him by surprise!
BEN: Strike while the pot is hot . . .

> BEN *puts his head under* CHARLOTTE'*s dress and disappears.*

CHARLOTTE: He won't know whether he's coming or going!
CATH HAGERTY: Wot do you think, Ben?

> BEN *mumbles something completely inaudible.*

CHARLOTTE: I think he's partial to the idea.

> CHARLOTTE *and* CATH HAGERTY *kiss, while* BEN *remains under wraps. A door opens and a shaft of light streams in. The* CAPTAIN *of the passenger ship* Venus, *enters. He is backlit and his presence is ominous. He is an English man of stature and authority. His dress is immaculate. He holds a whip. His voice is chilling.*

CAPTAIN: Are you are forgetting your post, Mr Kelly!

> *The three of them stop in their tracks.* BEN *takes his head from under* CHARLOTTE'*s dress.*

BEN: My post, Sir, is properly manned.

CATH HAGERTY *stifles a laugh.*

CAPTAIN: Get off those slags!
BEN: Sir!

BEN *stands up. The* CAPTAIN *grabs* CHARLOTTE *by her hair, pulling her head back.*

CAPTAIN: I'll teach you to lead my lads astray, Badger! A few days in the dark will douse your stinking spirits!

CHARLOTTE *glares at him.*

CHARLOTTE: Fuck off!

He pushes CHARLOTTE *forward, still holding her by the hair.*

CAPTAIN: You cussing little piece of whoredom. You think spreading your legs and whispering insurrection will do you any good! *(To* BEN, *referring to* CATH HAGERTY) Get that filth out of here! And get rid of that sprog as well.

BEN *picks up the baby and takes her and* CATH HAGERTY *out.*

CAPTAIN: Behave like a harlot, Charlotte, and you'll be treated like one! Is that what you want?
CHARLOTTE: Fuck off!
CAPTAIN: Only language you speak, isn't it?

He pushes CHARLOTTE *roughly over a wooden bench, and holds her face down, putting his whip down in the process.*

CAPTAIN: You're made to be shagged, Charlotte! That's all my men are after. Understand! Men will not mutiny for the likes of you! They're after a bit of hole that's all! Now move!

He pushes her up against a wall. With one hand he pulls up her skirt and unbuttons himself and readies himself to push into her from behind. She bites him. He yelps in pain.

CAPTAIN: Ahhh! Christ all fucking mighty! You hurt my hand you miserable moll! Kelly! Get in here! Teach you a lesson, you viperous little vixen! Kelly! I'll beat a lesson into you!

He holds her against the wall and raises his whip. BEN *enters.*

BEN: Is that the way to treat a mother, Sir? Mother with a newborn babe, not three days on the breast, Sir.

CAPTAIN: She's suckled every man on this tug! She's not worth the trouble of transportation. Pity the poor settler who's hired her for a servant. Here, do it for me, man.

> BEN KELLY *sniffs and stares at* CHARLOTTE *but does not move.*

CAPTAIN: What in the flaming pigs are you waiting for?!

BEN: It's just that I'm not sure, Sir. Not sure the lady likes the suggestion.

CAPTAIN: Are you trying to be comical, Mr Kelly?

BEN: I do like a good laugh, Sir. But in this case, I am genuine in my line of inquiry. Is the captain's proposal to your liking, Miss?

> CHARLOTTE *spits on the floor. The* CAPTAIN *looks from* BEN *to* CHARLOTTE *and back again.*

BEN: I think we can take that as a 'no', Sir.

CAPTAIN: Lash this 'lady', Kelly, or you'll find yourself in the dung pit!

> *The* CAPTAIN *starts to leave.* BEN *speaks very politely.*

BEN: Talking about shite, Sir, I think it's you that's in for the long drop.

> *The* CAPTAIN *stops and looks at him as if he's mad.*

CAPTAIN: *What?*

BEN: Door's locked, Sir.

> *A rhythmic and menacing drumbeat begins. Two* MASKED SAILORS *enter—one possibly dropping down on ropes from the ceiling. They move in on the* CAPTAIN *in a stylised, rhythmic stomp. The* CAPTAIN *starts to look panicked.*

CAPTAIN: What the breathing Jesus . . . Jesus Christ!

BEN: That's right, Sir. Mr Christ would be the only person to render you assistance at this juncture.

> BEN *grabs the* CAPTAIN*'s pistol from his waistband.*

CAPTAIN: You're an ignoramus, Kelly!

The CAPTAIN *attempts to leave.*

BEN: One more step, Sir, and you'll stop a shot quicker than you can say Jack Robinson.

CAPTAIN: Can't you see what you're in for?

BEN: What am I in for, Captain? Or more appropriately, what are you in for? What's the verdict, Charlotte?

CHARLOTTE *picks up the captain's whip.*

CHARLOTTE: A little lashing, Ben. Then a little ride in a longboat. With any crew wot are left loyal.

BEN: Which won't be many, Sir. One or two I'd say.

CAPTAIN: You'll be court-martialled, Kelly!

BEN: I don't think so, Sir. I will be dancing. Spread him!

The MASKED SAILORS *restrain him, taking an arm each.*

CHARLOTTE: Unwrap him first.

CAPTAIN: What?

The CAPTAIN *looks terrified.*

CHARLOTTE: I wanna see his white English bum! Besides, I rather fancy his frock coat!

The MASKED SAILORS *take off the captain's clothes, leaving only his long johns on.* CHARLOTTE *proceeds to put his clothes on. She looks dashing in his beautiful captain's coat and regalia.*

CAPTAIN: Please. Please don't do this. Don't hurt me, please. I have a wife and children.

The CAPTAIN *falls to his knees.*

BEN: We will be merciful, Sir.

CHARLOTTE: More merciful than you been to us, prick!

CHARLOTTE *takes the captain's whip—a cat-o'-nine-tails— and stands in front of him like a dominatrix.*

CHARLOTTE: Mind if I oblige, Ben?

BEN: She's very good at it, Sir.

CAPTAIN: Please . . . please don't hurt me.

> CHARLOTTE *runs the whip down his chest and through his legs.*

CHARLOTTE: I will be gentle. But you 'ave been a bad boy, 'aven't you?

> *Despite himself the* CAPTAIN *is terrified and aroused at the same time.*

CHARLOTTE: I said, 'aven't you!

CAPTAIN: Yes, yes I have . . .

CHARLOTTE: And you deserve to be punished. Don't you?

CAPTAIN: Yes. Yes I do.

CHARLOTTE: Tell the gentlemen of the jury wot a bad boy you been.

> *The* CAPTAIN *is shocked and aroused into submission and is silent.* CHARLOTTE *puts the handle of the whip through his legs again.*

CHARLOTTE: I said tell 'em!

BEN: Do what the lady says.

CHARLOTTE: Do it!

CAPTAIN: I . . . I deserve to be whipped, Madam.

CHARLOTTE: That's good. An' you deserve a cat-o'-nine-tails, don't you?

BEN: He deserves to be knackered!

CAPTAIN: Yes, Madam.

CHARLOTTE: An' I'm gonna give it to you, aren't I. Something your wife shoulda given you. You'd like that, wouldn't you?

> CHARLOTTE *continues to tantalise him with the whip.*

CAPTAIN: Yes . . . Yes I would . . .

CHARLOTTE: Show us his rump!

> *The* CAPTAIN *whimpers as his bare buttocks are revealed. He is lowered over the bench by the two* MASKED SAILORS *who then fade off.*

CHARLOTTE: Not a very pretty sight, is it?

CHARLOTTE *runs the handle of the whip over his buttocks and leans down and talks to him in a sonorous voice, which builds rapidly to a pitch.*

BEN: Puts me right off my breakfast.
CHARLOTTE: But you do deserve it, don't you?
CAPTAIN: Yes, yes I do.
CHARLOTTE: That's good. Say it again. An' say please.
CAPTAIN: Please, Madam.
CHARLOTTE: That's good. And again!
CAPTAIN: I deserve it, Madam.
CHARLOTTE: You do. An' again!
CAPTAIN: I deserve it, Madam!
CHARLOTTE: Say it again, fucker!
CAPTAIN: I deserve it!
CHARLOTTE: That's good, scum hole! And again!
CAPTAIN: I deserve it, Madam!
CHARLOTTE: Deserve wot, Captain?
CAPTAIN: To be punished, Madam.
CHARLOTTE: That's right, Madam!
CAPTAIN: That's right, Madam.
CHARLOTTE: Say yes, Madam!
CAPTAIN: Yes, Madam!
CHARLOTTE: Say please, Madam!
CAPTAIN: Please, Madam!
CHARLOTTE: Yes please, Madam!
CAPTAIN: Yes please, Madam!
CHARLOTTE: Yes please, Madam!
CAPTAIN: Yes please, Madam!
CHARLOTTE: Yes please, Madam!
CAPTAIN: Yes please, Madam! Yesssssssssssssssss!
CHARLOTTE: Yessssssssssssssssssss!

It reaches a climax. CHARLOTTE *raises the whip. Lighting change. Drumbeats. Blackout.*

Scene 2: Wellington Wharf, 1863

Sound of a ship's horn. A PORTER *enters, carrying a large theatrical trunk and a basket. Behind him, in full sail, is the actress,* MRS ADELAIDE FOLEY. *A newspaper billboard reads, 'Escaped Convict Who Whipped Sea Captain Re-sighted In North'.*

PORTER: Do you require a horse and cart, Ma'am?

ADELAIDE: I do indeed. And could you recommend a decent hotel? Something capacious. Last time I came to Wellington, I ended up in either an opium den or a brothel! In any case it was inconsolably small!

PORTER: There's the Thistle Inn, Ma'am, just opposite the public stocks, but that's not especially commodious. I would personally recommend The Empire Hotel, up on Willis Street. Dickey Dwyer runs a very nice establishment. Reading room, billiard room, lovely class of clientele.

ADELAIDE: Dickey's sounds divine! And could you also direct me to the portrait gallery of a Mr Richard Swan. We have some business together.

PORTER: Ah! Now that's easy, Ma'am. Mr Swan has premises over at Clay Point. A stone's throw from the hotel.

ADELAIDE: Magnificent!

PORTER: Have you any more baggage, Ma'am?

ADELAIDE: I have an entire wardrobe, Sir. Not to mention a couple of infuriatingly late performers, who've managed to get lost on a gangplank! Thank God I can see one of them now! The other one's probably fallen in the drink! Do come and see our entertainments. Royal Olympic Theatre, behind the Ship Hotel. Three nights only.

PORTER: I don't approve of theatricals, Ma'am. Devilism enacted on stage. This settlement has had a constant stream of vagabond Vaudevillians passing through it of late, creating all manner of licentious behaviour! What with liquor being passed around the pit and foul-mouthed debauchery, it's become offensive to ladies and gentlemen of the first quality!

ADELAIDE: My good man, let me inform you that my company could not be described as Vaudevillian. We have enacted our theatricals before the Queen! Not to mention the Princess

Royal. We perform Shakespeare, the most beautiful language in the world. I sing opera, superbly well I might add. And in addition, we delight with a small menagerie of animals. Everything, Sir, from the wild and ferocious Bengal leopard, to the twelfth wonder of the world, the Double-Headed Goat! So you see, Sir, it is manifestly absurd that you should find The Foley Theatrical Company threatening! Rather you should fight for a good seat!

PORTER: Forgive me, Madam! Heaven implore us. I had not recognised you! I most humbly beg your pardon, Mrs Foley.

ADELAIDE *smiles charmingly.*

ADELAIDE: Forgiven!

PORTER: My dear, Mrs Foley, I have seen you perform on two marvellous occasions, and each time you have added considerable class to our young colony!

ADELAIDE: How kind. Now run along and get that leading man off the gangplank. He's about to fall over his wig box!

PORTER: Pleasure, Mrs Foley. Pleasure. Truly a pleasure.

ADELAIDE: I'm so glad!

CAMERON CARRUTHERS *struggles on with several small cases.*

ADELAIDE: Good God, Cameron, you look as if you're about to expire!

CAMERON: Concerts in the colonies, Adelaide, are not my idea of a capital time! Bloody idiot I was to be talked into this! And if I never see the *S.S. Stormbird* again I'll be damn grateful! Ghastly crossing and the digs are downright common!

ADELAIDE: Come, come, where's your sense of adventure?

CAMERON: Back in England with a weekly repertory and a decent bit of Yorkshire pud! Good God, look at that landscape. Not a soul alive and hedged in by hills! Bottom of the bloody world!

The PORTER *relieves* CAMERON *of the bags.*

ADELAIDE: Where on earth is Kathryn?

CAMERON: Last time I saw her, she was surrounded by six randy sailors.

ADELAIDE: That's a fine predicament to leave your fiancée in! You might at least have acted the gentleman and fought them off.

CAMERON: Kathryn's more than capable of shoving them overboard.

ADELAIDE: And *don't* think I didn't see you eyeing up a young colonial thing yourself.

CAMERON: Adelaide, Adelaide, you don't miss a trick do you. I was admiring her hair!

ADELAIDE: You were admiring her bosom!

CAMERON *smiles charmingly.*

CAMERON: And I'm admiring yours now.

ADELAIDE: You never change do you.

CAMERON: Would you want me to?

ADELAIDE *smiles, despite herself.*

ADELAIDE: Probably not.

CAMERON *taps his pockets.*

CAMERON: Where'd I put that damn flask?

CAMERON *pulls out a whisky flask and takes a swig.*

ADELAIDE: That's your trouble, Cameron. Too much spirit and not enough pluck!

CAMERON: You do go on, Adelaide.

ADELAIDE: Precious little good it does!

CAMERON: Ah, here she is!

KATHRYN *enters. She is a beautiful woman in her late 30s. Her clothes have a look of fashion, theatricality and flair.*

ADELAIDE: Kathryn where have you been? We're forever waiting, it's maddening.

KATHRYN *looks around, delighted.*

KATHRYN: Oh what light! What exquisite light! We have arrived in heaven, surely!

CAMERON: Kathryn, your brain has been sodden by that cheerless little boat ride! What nautical nonsense! Mind you, after that crossing, any bit of land would be a blessing! Talk about tempests!

KATHRYN: 'When the shore is won at last, who can remember the billows past!'

CAMERON: No use quoting Swinburne at me! It was a horrid little hulk and I hope I never have to see it again!

KATHRYN: Oh, Cammy, how can you be so cruelly ungrateful to that virtuous vessel! That gallant little barque that bore us here. She rose against the salt like a lioness protecting her young. You really are a philistine!

CAMERON: Yes, but a very charming one!

ADELAIDE: Perhaps we could *attempt* to meet Mr Swan before midnight.

CAMERON: Yes, and I do hope he's not another vapid, talent-free, vanity queen who can't act his way out of a paper bag!

ADELAIDE: Cameron darling, every support actor I've ever had can act! Eventually.

CAMERON: I rest my case!

ADELAIDE: Shall we go?

CAMERON: Yes, let us depart this shapeless shore!

KATHRYN: Farewell then, thou dark and deep blue ocean. Ta ta my tireless little tugboat. Parting is such sorrow, sorrow. God I'm absolutely starving. What are we waiting for?

She smiles delightfully at CAMERON *and* ADELAIDE *who walk off. The* PORTER *is left to pick up a mountain of luggage.* KATHRYN *picks up a couple of small bags. She stops at the newspaper stand and reads the billboard of the* Independent.

KATHRYN: Oh, do look at the headlines, how exciting! Escaped Convict Who Whipped Sea Captain Re-sighted in North! How very dramatic!

PORTER: They've been looking for that felon for years, Miss. She's been on the loose for a decade now. Very depraved piece of work! Murderer, thief, prostitute! You name it! They think she's hiding out with the natives. They say she actually stripped the captain and whipped his bare . . . his bare . . .

He can't quite say the word. Pause.

KATHRYN: Bare what?
PORTER: Bottom.

> KATHRYN *can't help but find this amusing.*

KATHRYN: Oh really?
PORTER: She stripped him of his clothes and then used them to outfit herself!
KATHRYN: How very Shakespearean!

> *She smiles charmingly and exits. The* PORTER *stands there with his mountain of baggage. He calls after* KATHRYN.

PORTER: Miss! Are there any seats left for tonight's performance?

Scene 3: Richard Swan's Portrait Gallery

RICHARD SWAN, *a professional photographer in his early 30s, is fiddling with a camera on a wooden tripod. He is a handsome, enthusiastic man, whose hair and dress are slightly dishevelled, as if he has dressed very hastily. He brims with energy. His studio also has a wooden chair with several frames leaning against it. A stereoscope sits on the chair.*

ADELAIDE *enters.* RICHARD *doesn't see her until she speaks. He is holding a glass photographic plate up to the light.*

ADELAIDE: Mr Richard Swan?

> RICHARD *turns around.*

RICHARD: Oh, I didn't hear you come in! I was completely absorbed in this latest apparatus from London. It's a carte de visite camera, *(He taps the camera.)* capable of taking four pictures in one sitting! So if it's a portrait you're after, I highly recommend it!
ADELAIDE: I'm after an actor, Mr Swan! And Mr James Marriot recommended you.
RICHARD: Marriot! Oh yes, I've performed with Marriot several times. Great comic actor! Fine timing.
ADELAIDE: Adelaide Foley. Delighted to meet you.
RICHARD: *The* Mrs Foley? The delight is all mine! Foley's Circus?

I've seen it of course.

ADELAIDE: My husband manages the circus side of the business, Mr Swan. We tend to perform rather separately these days. I'm here at the moment with a much smaller dramatic company. And I'm looking for an actor to join our North Island tour—Wellington, Napier, Wanganui, Auckland. Six weeks. And a share of the proceeds. It appears you have a formidable reputation.

RICHARD: I am indeed honoured, Mrs Foley!

ADELAIDE: You are a much younger-looking man than I expected. And much more handsome. I should be delighted if you'd join us.

RICHARD: Mrs Foley, I would normally leap at the chance of performing in such illustrious company! But the photographic business is fairly booming at the moment. Just started to take off in fact, with this new carte de visite craze! I couldn't possibly leave Wellington.

ADELAIDE: Perhaps you'd like to come and see us perform, Mr Swan, before making any rash decisions. *(She looks around.)* Marvellous equipment you have. *(She picks up the stereoscope.)* I've always been fascinated by photographic portraiture. What is this curious piece, Mr Swan?

RICHARD: Ah! Now that 'curious piece' is the second new innovation just arrived from England! It's a stereoscope, Mrs Foley! Fantastic invention!

>   RICHARD *picks up a stereoscopic card.*

RICHARD: How it works is like this, a person or a pictorial view, is photographed from two different angles. It uses a special camera, which employs two lenses. And when the image is developed, it's printed onto a stiff card, three and a half inches by seven inches . . .

>   ADELAIDE *is suddenly very interested.*

ADELAIDE: How fascinating . . .
RICHARD: Here. Have a look.

>   RICHARD *hands her the stereoscope and she looks through it as he slips the card into the viewfinder. He's very close to her, although only she is really conscious of it.*

RICHARD: The card is slipped into the stereoscope, like so, then it optically merges the two images, and when viewed through the apparatus, it gives the illusion of a third dimension! Fantastic isn't it!

ADELAIDE: Fantastic.

RICHARD: Of course they can now also be reproduced on the wet plate.

ADELAIDE: Can they indeed?

RICHARD: And this makes them much more available.

ADELAIDE: Fascinating.

RICHARD: So you see, Mrs Foley, this new craze means that the average colonist can send his friends back home faithful sketches of the land he lives in!

ADELAIDE: Perfect!

RICHARD: On a far grander scale, it means that those who lack the daring to visit the ruins of antique architecture, for example, can view the remnants of lost civilisations and look first-hand at the genius of ages past, without moving an inch from their armchair!

ADELAIDE: How exciting your work must be, Mr Swan.

RICHARD: Where did you say you were performing?

ADELAIDE: Royal Olympic Theatre.

RICHARD: Ah, I photographed the Royal Olympic just recently! It was published in *Vanity Fair*. *(He picks up a copy.)* Here you are you see, it's a sort of panorama, taken from Willis Street and looking down Manners. Fine theatre.

ADELAIDE *looks at the photograph and smiles charmingly.*

ADELAIDE: I see you are a very talented artiste, Mr Swan. I'm sure you could excel at anything you put your hand to.

RICHARD: Coming from you, Mrs Foley, that is indeed a compliment.

ADELAIDE: I insist that you come and see the show, Mr Swan, I shall leave your name at the door.

RICHARD: I shall be delighted to see you perform, as always.

ADELAIDE: Till then.

ADELAIDE *leaves.*

Scene 4: Royal Olympic Theatre—Wellington

ADELAIDE *is at the back of the stage singing to her 'audience' who we do not see this time. Her back is to the real audience. The singing is heard in the distance.*

KATHRYN *is alone in the dressing room, reciting a piece of poetry. She looks luminous in a half light. With* ADELAIDE *onstage in the background. (Lighting should suggest oil lamps on the stage and a combination of candles and oil lamps in the auditorium.)*

KATHRYN: 'Why wilt thou follow lesser loves? Are thine too weak to bear these hands and lips of mine? I charge thee for my life's sake, O too sweet to crush love with thy cruel faultless feet, I charge thee keep thy lips from hers or his, sweetest, till theirs be sweeter than my kiss.'

> CAMERON *enters and watches her. They speak in muted backstage voices.*

CAMERON: Exquisite! Such sweet sonorous tones. You are simply a goddess. My sexy, sensuous, little Goddess! They're piled to the ceiling out there. Lapping it up! I adore it when you spout poetry.

KATHRYN: Swinburne.

CAMERON: A debauched chap if ever there was one! You do know what that poem's about don't you? It's a sadistic piece of sapphism.

KATHRYN: What rubbish!

CAMERON: The *Times* critic said so! I'm simply quoting the *Times!*

KATHRYN: Darling, it is a poet's licence to explore love and sex in all its prettiness and pain. How can you possibly be so reductive about such a beautiful piece of poetry?

CAMERON: Ah! That's the kind of sentiment that comes from reading Swinburne. He's a randy young bugger.

KATHRYN: Au contraire. I read Swinburne *because* I hold such sentiments. Anyway, I thought him a real gentleman when I met him. Not at all the licentious laureate he's made out to be.

CAMERON: Well, I for one have no objection to you exploring

love and sex, as long as you explore it with me. I don't think these colonials realise what a smutty little girl you are underneath it all.

KATHRYN: I should think they'd be delighted. They're probably like that themselves in the privacy of their own bedrooms.

CAMERON: No, I'm quite sure they don't copulate. That's why the town is so deserted.

He goes over to her and starts kissing her.

CAMERON: Now I *don't* think you should argue with me any more.

KATHRYN *responds between kisses.*

KATHRYN: It's you that argues with *me.*

CAMERON: Oh, Kathryn, Kathryn. You *are* beautiful. I do adore you. You are my absolute Goddess. You are all my fantasies rolled into one. You are the most divinely beautiful woman . . .

KATHRYN: Cammy, we'll miss the curtain call . . .

CAMERON *starts kissing her more frantically, gabbling Swinburne at the same time.*

CAMERON: Oh, Kathryn . . . 'My life is bitter with thy love, thine eyes blind me, thy tresses burn me, thy sharp sighs divide my flesh and spirit with soft sound, and my blood strengthens and my veins abound. I pray thee sigh not, speak not, draw not breath' . . . ahh . . . aah . . . aah! Oh fuck!

KATHRYN: Cammy, this is not the time or the place.

CAMERON *puts his arms around her.*

CAMERON: I'm sorry darling, I'm a pig, I know it. I'll make it up to you I promise.

KATHRYN: If only you made it up to me at the appropriate times!

Sound of applause in the background. ADELAIDE *bows several times.*

CAMERON: Damn! We missed the curtain call.

KATHRYN: And whose fault is that?

CAMERON: Mine. I'll face the music.

He comes over to her.

CAMERON: The moment we get back to England we shall set our wedding date. Not a second later!

KATHRYN: Are you sure it's not just a mistress you want?

CAMERON: Darling, we'd do it here, but I simply couldn't bear getting married in the colonies.

KATHRYN: I should think it very romantic. Why, here one could do anything.

> *Sound of applause in the background.* ADELAIDE *sweeps in, in full regalia.*

ADELAIDE: You missed the curtain call! *Where were* you?

CAMERON: Darling, you were splendid tonight! You deserved all the accolades! Sublime! No point in us coming on! Mere mortals that we are. Trundling onto the boards, fading into the curtains!

ADELAIDE: I was in full form, I must say! But I *don't* think that's the reason you didn't come on!

> CAMERON *sees* RICHARD SWAN *coming in with an armful of flowers.*

CAMERON: No, but it should've been. Oh look! You have an admirer!

> ADELAIDE *sees* RICHARD *and beams.*

CAMERON: Thank God!

ADELAIDE: Mr Swan! How lovely of you to come!

RICHARD: Mrs Foley. You were sublime. Utterly, unspeakably sublime.

CAMERON: See what I mean?

RICHARD: You were magic. Sheer magic.

> ADELAIDE *is in her element.*

ADELAIDE: Thank you. Thank you so much. Where were you sitting?

RICHARD: Words cannot express it. You inspired universal admiration! The public adored you. And you had the 14th Regiment eating out of your palm.

ADELAIDE: You were a lovely audience. You really were.

RICHARD: We were transported by you!

ADELAIDE: I'm so glad.

RICHARD: I've reconsidered your offer. I'll come! I simply must! I knew it when you performed Viola! And when you sang the Mozart, well, I was already waiting in the wings!

ADELAIDE: I am delighted, Mr Swan! Truly delighted.

RICHARD: My business partner can hold the fort while I'm away. And I can combine it with my photographic interests. I'll bring some equipment with me and make some scenic excursions for the cartes de visite. And we'll do some publicity shots for the company as well.

ADELAIDE: How simply marvellous. Isn't it, Cameron?

CAMERON: Yes marvellous.

RICHARD: Oh! These are for you.

> RICHARD *hands over the flowers.*

ADELAIDE: Thank you. They are absolutely darling. Aren't they, Cameron?

CAMERON: Darling.

> CAMERON *comes over and introduces himself.*

CAMERON: Cameron Carruthers.

> *He shakes* RICHARD's *hand.*

RICHARD: Richard Swan. She was superb, wasn't she!

> *He looks at* ADELAIDE, *still shaking* CAMERON's *hand.*

RICHARD: She really was.

> CAMERON *is a little piqued at his dismissal.*

CAMERON: Yes she was. And this is Kathryn Horton. Also marvellous.

KATHRYN: Pleased to meet you, Mr Swan.

RICHARD: Thoroughly honoured! You were magnificent as well.

> *He shakes* KATHRYN's *hand.*

CAMERON: Not the most glamorous tour we've done! Regimental Dramatic Society in Napier, Albert Barracks in Auckland, and the Regimental Dramatic Society in Wanganui. Very exciting don't you think!

ADELAIDE *flashes* CAMERON *an irritated look and then smiles back to* RICHARD.

ADELAIDE: We have the privilege of performing to Governor Grey in Auckland, Mr Swan. And that is a rare honour indeed!

RICHARD: Indeed, Mrs Foley.

CAMERON: We're catching the schooner at sparrow's fart. 7am!

RICHARD: I shall be there at six! Thank you. Thank you.

RICHARD *waves to the other two and leaves.*

CAMERON: Enthusiastic little man, isn't he!

ADELAIDE: I thought him charming.

CAMERON *gets his whisky flask out.*

CAMERON: Let's pray he's better than the last one. Your penchant for young leading idiots will ruin us!

ADELAIDE: He's exceptionally talented, I could see it in his face.

CAMERON: It wasn't his face you were looking at.

ADELAIDE: Pardon?

CAMERON: Anyone for a nightcap?

KATHRYN: Cammy, don't drink any more tonight. Please.

CAMERON: Kathryn darling, it's just a little after-show wind down. What could be wrong with that? Just a little one, I promise. Very little. Teeny, teeny weeny.

KATHRYN *sighs. She proceeds to take off her costume.*

Scene 5: Schooner—Waitemata Harbour

Ship's horn. Night-time, stars. ADELAIDE *and* RICHARD *wander on deck.*

ADELAIDE: Oh yes, Mr Swan! I've worked with Mrs Siddons on several occasions, and the great actor, Henry Irving. And, of course, Disraeli and Browning are among our house guests in London. Darling Dizzy, he's a heaven-born artist. Have you read his novels?

RICHARD: Not yet.

ADELAIDE: Then you have a treat in store. Can anyone with a pictorial sense fail to be delighted by their pageantry!

RICHARD *laughs, thoroughly charmed by her.*

RICHARD: Probably not!

Pause.

ADELAIDE: I love sailing into a harbour at night. Don't you? All those little lights. Twinkling away like stars. It's so romantic, Richard.

Pause.

ADELAIDE: May I call you, Richard?

RICHARD: Yes . . . Yes, of course.

ADELAIDE: Do *you* find it romantic?

RICHARD: Mmm . . . yes. Now, that island over there! That's an extinct volcano! Can you believe that? You wouldn't get that in England. You really wouldn't. It deserves be photographed. Perfect carte de visite. Landmark of the capital. Conical shape. Almost symmetrical. Interesting vegetation . . . Did you know that the North Island at this point is only six miles wide? It really is a narrow isthmus . . . And few settlements can boast such picturesque scenery don't you think? . . . In fact I suggest a photographic excursion around the harbour . . . publicity pictures would surely be enhanced by . . .

ADELAIDE: Do I make you nervous, Mr Swan?

Pause.

RICHARD: You make my thoughts tumble over themselves, Mrs Foley.

ADELAIDE: Adelaide.

RICHARD: Adelaide. I have to confess to never being so nervous as when I stepped out on that stage with you last night.

ADELAIDE: You looked in perfect composure.

RICHARD: The garrison didn't seem to mind. Of course they had eyes only for you. You could've been acting with a paper bag!

ADELAIDE: I normally *do* act with a paper bag!

RICHARD: You were sublime. And when you sang! Your voice was like a silver river flowing over gold stones.

ADELAIDE: Oh, Richard, you are like a refreshing breath of theatrical air. And you're also a very fine actor.
RICHARD: Thank you.

> *Pause.* ADELAIDE's *voice is sonorous. She is enjoying the knowledge that she does indeed make him nervous.*

ADELAIDE: Do I still make you nervous?
RICHARD: In Baillie's words, 'I shrunk at first in awe; but when she smiled, for so she did, to see me thus abashed, methought I could have compassed sea and land to do her bidding.'
ADELAIDE: Then I am very flattered. You should have more confidence, Richard. You have a beautiful voice. Beautiful eyes . . . Beautiful hands . . .
RICHARD: Now I really am shy.
ADELAIDE: And your boyish shyness is one of the most charming things about you.
RICHARD: I am astonished that you think so . . .
ADELAIDE: I do. And you are sensitive and poetic and very, very . . .

> ADELAIDE *is about to lean in and give him a kiss, when* CAMERON *comes on.*

CAMERON: Oh, don't mind me! Just talking to the captain! Capital fellow! Drinks more than I do! Reckons we should be docked in a minute. I got all the local goss! Fact is, it's a bit of a bloody bun fight up here! Your Governor Grey's ordered all natives north of the river to either throw in their lot with the Queen, or push off down south! Some of the natives got a bit uppity. Few fisticuffs flying around. Garrison's on red alert. Great timing, Adelaide! Capital time to come!
ADELAIDE: Then I'm sure the garrison will appreciate some fine entertainments, Cameron. Now if we're about to disembark wouldn't you think it wise to find Kathryn?
CAMERON: Last time I saw Kathryn she was looking like the virgin of the sun! Steering the ship to shore! She had the midshipman in tow! Positively panting at her feet, teaching her how to hold the wheel! That's his story anyway and he's sticking to it! Damn fine-looking volcano that!

Scene 6: Manukau Harbour—Auckland

Sound of waves, seagulls. KATHRYN *comes on carrying* RICHARD's *camera on its wooden tripod. She is talking to the others who are a few paces behind her.*

KATHRYN: What about over here? It looks splendid with the waves in the background.

CAMERON: Not another one, surely?

KATHRYN *walks around, observing positions.*

KATHRYN: Oh, look at these crimson blossoms. It's so full of luxuriant growth, Richard.

RICHARD: It's richly alluvial. The native flora here simply flourishes.

CAMERON: We've taken enough portraitures to fill an entire album.

KATHRYN: Those trees are like giants.

RICHARD: Magnificent aren't they? Hundreds and thousands of years old.

CAMERON: Do let's be done with it, darling.

ADELAIDE: Yes, we've left the animals at the barracks, remember? They're probably dying of thirst.

CAMERON: I've got an ill feeling about this place . . .

KATHRYN: Just one more please. One of the three of you together. And don't move this time, Cammy! Or we'll have to put a steel rod down your back.

CAMERON: Oh, heaven preserve us!

KATHRYN: Is this light good, Richard? And did you say the sun behind? Or the sun in front? I should think we'll lose it altogether soon.

RICHARD: It's better further down I think. We'll check.

The three of them walk off, leaving KATHRYN *fiddling with the camera.*

CAMERON, *off*: Just take the damn thing, please! Our driver's probably got bored dilly and gone back to Auckland! Surely you've got your year's quota, Swan!

KATHRYN: He has, but I want one more! So don't be such an unco-operative brute! There. That's good there! Just move back one more step . . . And one more again.

CAMERON, *off*: One more again and we'll end up in the bloody
    drink!
RICHARD, *off*: Mind your step. There are great jungles of flax.
ADELAIDE: Ow! I've twisted my ankle.
CAMERON: Oh, that's all we need. A limping Viola.
ADELAIDE: Thanks for that sympathy, Cameron!
RICHARD, *to* KATHRYN: Remember what I told you. Keep the sun
    behind you, and angle it more.
KATHRYN: Sorry. I forgot! It was better over there! Oh this setting
    is so picturesque. It'll make a handsome portraiture.
CAMERON, *off*: Oh, for goodness sake, Kathryn! Call us when you're
    ready! Better still, don't call us and we won't call you!
KATHRYN: Get ready to be posed.
ADELAIDE, *off*: Ow!

> *The sound of distant drums, chants.*

RICHARD, *off*: Adelaide. You've hurt yourself.
ADELAIDE, *off*: I think I've sprained my ankle.

> KATHRYN *goes back to the camera. Sounds of the others*
> *talking in the background, about* ADELAIDE*'s ankle.*

RICHARD, *off*: Let me take a look at it.
ADELAIDE, *off*: Oh dear, it's very painful.
CAMERON, *off*: What in God's name is that sound?

> *The distant drums continue.* KATHRYN *angles the camera*
> *around.* CHARLOTTE *silently emerges from the trees.*
> KATHRYN *places the camera in the new position, and fiddles*
> *around with it for a moment. She looks down at the camera*
> *and fiddles with it as she speaks.*

KATHRYN: I've got it now. Yes that's marvellous. Oh, but I do think
    we ought to hurry! The shadows are starting to . . .

> *As she raises her gaze, she finds herself staring, face to face*
> *with* CHARLOTTE. *There is a strange sense of suspended*
> *animation.* KATHRYN *is too shocked to speak or move. She*
> *stands stock-still, for what seems an eternity. They are both*
> *awestruck by the other. Two strangers from foreign lands.*
> CHARLOTTE *looks older than when we last saw her. She is*
> *still wearing the captain's frock coat, but it is very much*

faded and worn. She has a rakish, suntanned, outdoor look about her. KATHRYN swallows, transfixed. Her voice is soft, almost whispered.

KATHRYN: What are you?

Pause.

CAMERON: Katie, let's stop for the day, for God's sake!

CAMERON's voice breaks the strange mood. KATHRYN glances back at the others and looks for a moment as though she's about to move. She puts her hand out to the camera to steady herself. CHARLOTTE produces a pistol and trains it on KATHRYN. Her voice is low and threatening.

CHARLOTTE: *Don't move!*

In her shock at seeing the pistol, KATHRYN accidentally hits the camera button, taking a photo of CHARLOTTE in the process. She virtually whispers in fear. CHARLOTTE doesn't respond. Just keeps the pistol steadily trained on KATHRYN.

KATHRYN: Don't think you can intimidate me with that . . . that thing . . .

LUCY, a ten-year-old child, emerges from the trees. She comes and stands next to CHARLOTTE and sticks her thumb in her mouth. She is a barefooted, dark-skinned child, with huge, cavernous eyes. KATHRYN looks from one to the other. RICHARD's voice gets closer.

RICHARD, *off*: We need to relocate. We're losing light.

CHARLOTTE slowly and deliberately puts the pistol away.

CHARLOTTE: Breathe a word. You'll regret it.
RICHARD: Are you sure you're alright, Adelaide?
ADELAIDE: Yes . . . yes, I think so.
CAMERON: Then hadn't we better head back.
ADELAIDE: Yes, I should think I've had enough for one day.
RICHARD: Yes, of course you have.

They all emerge about the same time, ADELAIDE limping ever so slightly.

CAMERON: Good God, we've got company. And I thought we were in the middle of the wop wops!

RICHARD: We are. I didn't think there was a farmhouse in miles. Do you live in these parts?

> CHARLOTTE *doesn't respond.* ADELAIDE *looks at* KATHRYN.

ADELAIDE: Does she speak English?

KATHRYN: Yes, she's . . . she's from the local mission station. Further south . . . Papakura. Isn't it?

> *Pause.*

CHARLOTTE: Yeah.

> *The others look uncomfortable in* CHARLOTTE'S *company and no one quite knows what to say. Silence. Then they all gabble over one another, but no one moves.*

RICHARD: We ought to head back to our driver.

ADELAIDE: Yes, if we're to reach Auckland by midnight!

RICHARD: We're performers you see. We were just taking photographic portraitures of our . . .

CHARLOTTE: Got any liquor?

> *They all shut up. Silence.*

CHARLOTTE: I said, got any liquor!

> CAMERON *and* KATHRYN *speak at once.*

CAMERON: No!

KATHRYN: Yes!

SWAN: I thought you had a whole flask, Cameron.

CAMERON: Did you really?

CHARLOTTE: Give it!

CAMERON: I most certainly will not! Who on earth do you think you are!

> CHARLOTTE *gives him a threatening look and then comes over to him in a menacing fashion.*

CHARLOTTE: I said *give it!*

> *Silence.*

Kathryn: Give it to her, Cameron!

> Cameron *senses that it's better to and hands over his flask.*
> Charlotte *takes a swig, then pockets it. Silence.* Richard
> *breaks it.*

Richard: Well, I really do think we ought to head back!

Adelaide: That's a very good idea I think.

> *They make moves.*

Charlotte: Won't get far tonight.

Adelaide: Why ever not?

> *The drums and chant intensify.*

Charlotte: Fightin' down on Great South Road.

Richard: I can't believe that. There was no sign of it earlier on.

Charlotte: If that were yor driver wot was waitin', he's long gone.
Fled to save his own skin.

Cameron: Cowardly piglet!

Richard: I can't understand it. There was simply no sign of it!

> *Sound of gunfire.*

Adelaide: But there is now I think!

Cameron: Oh, that's bloody marvellous, Swan! We're bloody
stranded on the bloody Antipodean shoreline, and it's your
bloody fault! I told you there was unrest in the area.

Richard: Everyone said it was a storm in a teacup!

> Kathryn *addresses* Charlotte.

Kathryn: Is there another means out of here?

Charlotte: Follow the coast. Then up Wairoa Road.

Richard: Wairoa Road. There's an Inn there, with a store and
lodgings. We could get a coach back to Auckland.

Charlotte: Tide's comin' in. Too dangerous.

Richard: Yes, she's right. Better wait till low tide.

Charlotte: Gotta know where the road starts. Where to cut up
from the rocks.

Cameron: I vote we go back the way we came!

Charlotte: Natives don't take kindly to white folk.

Adelaide: I can't walk any more.

RICHARD: No. Best if we camp on the beach and tackle the coast in the morning.

CAMERON: I'm not sleeping on a bloody beach!

ADELAIDE: Well, I'm not damaging this ankle. I've got to perform tomorrow night.

KATHRYN: We haven't much choice.

RICHARD: It wouldn't be the first time I've slept under the stars. I've done it often enough on my photographic excursions.

CAMERON: I'm sure you have! Seeing as your avocation seems to be little more than a series of holidays!

RICHARD: What are you implying, Carruthers?

CAMERON: Simply old chap, that some of us prefer a comfortable bed, when a professional engagement is forthcoming!

ADELAIDE, *interrupting quickly:* I suggest we find some firewood, and do what Richard says!

RICHARD: Yes, we should build a fire.

CAMERON: We've no food to cook on it, so I don't know what the point is!

ADELAIDE: It will keep us warm. If nothing else!

CAMERON *addresses* CHARLOTTE.

CAMERON: I don't suppose you've got any provisions?

ADELAIDE: Yes, you see, because it was simply an afternoon's excursion and we didn't pack a single sandwich.

CHARLOTTE *scoffs.*

CHARLOTTE: Wot d'you think this is? A bed and breakfast?

CAMERON: Yes. I had thought it was. You mean to say it's not?

CHARLOTTE: Why would I help the likes of you?

CHARLOTTE *leaves.* LUCY *stays and watches them.*

CHARLOTTE, *from off:* Lucy!

LUCY *leaves.*

CAMERON: That would have to be the most miserably wretched object I've ever come across!

ADELAIDE: She wasn't exactly ladylike.

CAMERON: If we listen to her, we're damned! Go one way, we're lost. Go the other way, we're shot. Charming!

RICHARD: We should attempt to keep our spirits up.

CAMERON: I don't trust that fishwife. She'll sell us to the natives and we'll end up as someone's supper! They're cannibalistic by nature you know.

RICHARD: Regard it as an adventure, Carruthers. We'll have enthralling tales to tell our friends back home.

ADELAIDE *is shivering.*

CAMERON: If we ever get back home! Good God, girl, you're shivering. Here, have this.

He starts to take his coat off.

RICHARD: It's alright, Carruthers. I'll take care of her!

RICHARD *gets his coat off faster and* CAMERON *relents, glaring at* RICHARD *as he speaks.*

CAMERON: Will you indeed?

RICHARD: Yes.

Pause.

CAMERON: Then I shall take a piss!

ADELAIDE *interrupts hurriedly.*

ADELAIDE: Perhaps you should light the fire, Cameron!

KATHRYN *looks around, tense.*

CAMERON: Fire. Yes . . . *(Glares at* RICHARD.*)* Something manly. Situation obviously requires it.

KATHRYN: It's getting dark . . . the light is soft to sight . . .

CAMERON *searches his pockets.*

CAMERON: Damn! I had some flint here. Can't understand that. I lit a pipe earlier on. Bugger! Bugger! Bugger!

RICHARD: Can't even get up a fire, eh, Carruthers?

CAMERON *is irate, but hides it in sarcasm. He takes* RICHARD *aside, an avuncular arm around his shoulder.*

CAMERON: Quick off the mark old boy, but a word of advice. If you want to get a matrimonial leg over, you have to realise the old girl likes a winner. You're dealing with a thoroughbred, man. A real racehorse. And she doesn't bugger about with bad riders! Time it carefully, old son. *(Slaps* RICHARD *on the back.)* Otherwise the pistol will go off and you'll be left sitting at the starting line. Looking like a complete prat!

RICHARD: Is that the only way you can speak of women? As livestock!

CAMERON: She's a woman of the world man! She likes quality.

RICHARD: I find you a vulgar bore, Carruthers!

CAMERON: And you, my dear chappy, are a poor excuse for a paramour. Now bugger off and find some flint.

RICHARD: I shall fetch some ferns for sleeping!

He goes off.

CAMERON: Idiot!

ADELAIDE: Calm down, Cameron! You look a picture of disgruntlement.

CAMERON *sits looking dejected.*

CAMERON: If it wasn't for him, we wouldn't be here, sans fire, in the first place! I can't even light a sodding pipe!

KATHRYN *looks tensely around her. She thinks she hears something behind them.*

KATHRYN: What was that?

ADELAIDE: Oh God it's starting to swell.

KATHRYN: I heard something!

CAMERON: What is it, Kathryn?

ADELAIDE: I shall be awake all night.

Sound of a morepork. She stands looking tense and worried.

KATHRYN: . . . Midnight and noon have a ghostly tune . . .

CAMERON: Cheerless little place isn't it?

Scene 7: Stream—Manukau Harbour

Sound of early morning birds—it is still quite dark. Charlotte *is washing Lucy's face very tenderly. They speak in Maori.* Kathryn *enters with a water flask and a lantern. She stands watching* Charlotte *for a second.*

LUCY: Kei te makariri. (It's cold.)

CHARLOTTE: Kaua e rori rori. (Don't be silly.)

LUCY: Kei te pirangi au ki te mahi takaro. (I want to go and play.)

CHARLOTTE: Au ringaringa. (Hands.) Ka pai. Ka pai tena. (That's good.)

KATHRYN: I know who you are.

> CHARLOTTE *stops, mid-action, but doesn't look back at* KATHRYN. *She wipes her mouth with the back of her hand. She doesn't say anything.*

KATHRYN: I'm surprised you didn't murder us in our beds!

CHARLOTTE, *scoffs*: Wasn't half tempted.

KATHRYN: Yet something preserved you from committing yet another crime.

CHARLOTTE: Dunno wot you talking about.

KATHRYN: I think you do.

CHARLOTTE, *to* LUCY: Haere atu. *(To* KATHRYN.*)* Ain't committed no crime.

KATHRYN: There's a large reward on your head. Very large, in fact.

CHARLOTTE: I must be famous then, mustn't I?

KATHRYN: Infamous actually.

> CHARLOTTE *walks over to her.*

CHARLOTTE: I think you're mistaking me for someone else.

KATHRYN: I don't think so.

> CHARLOTTE *grabs her in a threatening manner.*

CHARLOTTE: I'll have kill you then, won't I? Stop you tellin' the authorities. How'd you like to go then? Bullet through the 'eart? Or gutted an' quartered? Take your pick.

KATHRYN: Very kind of you to give me the choice.

CHARLOTTE: Can't take no risks!

KATHRYN: I won't tell anyone, I promise. Providing you lead us out of here.

CHARLOTTE: That's comical that is! You tryin' a' do a lay wi' me.

KATHRYN: Clearly you have the advantage. You have the privilege of naming your price. What would you charge for such a service?

> *Pause.* CHARLOTTE *lets her go. She looks back in the direction of the others.*

CHARLOTTE: Your cohorts seem to be sleeping soundly. Did you sleep soundly?

KATHRYN: Yes I did, thank you. Are you a murderess or a thief?

CHARLOTTE: I live here now in peace with the natives.

KATHRYN: Yet you stole my fiancé's flint!

> CHARLOTTE *smiles.*

CHARLOTTE: Force of habit. Dies hard.

> CHARLOTTE *throws it back to her.*

KATHRYN: Then if you won't tell me your crime, I shall have to think the worst of you.

CHARLOTTE: My crime was not being born flush in the pocket. Like you was.

KATHRYN: Poverty is no excuse for criminal behaviour.

> CHARLOTTE *scoffs.*

CHARLOTTE: Is that so!

KATHRYN: The authorities will catch up with you.

CHARLOTTE: I'm safe here 'mongst the Maori. Only ones ever helped the likes of me.

KATHRYN: But you won't be safe for much longer will you? Not if the Crown pushes all the natives south of the river.

> *Silence.* CHARLOTTE *is thinking.*

KATHRYN: Well?

CHARLOTTE: Tell you wot I'll do. I'll lead you up to the Traveller's Rest. Get you there nice an' safe like.

KATHRYN: I knew we could come to some arrangement.

CHARLOTTE: An' for that, you hand over twenty guineas.

KATHRYN: Twenty!

CHARLOTTE: An' you gimme them papers you use when you catch the sailing ships.

KATHRYN: My passport! That's flatly impossible.

CHARLOTTE: Oh, an' another thing. Not a word to your cohorts.

KATHRYN: You obviously take me for a complete fool!

CHARLOTTE: No skin off my nose. Stay here an' starve then.

> CHARLOTTE *starts to go.*

KATHRYN: Wait! Wait a minute! How soon could we leave?

> CHARLOTTE *smiles at her.*

CHARLOTTE: Second thoughts then 'ave we?

Scene 8: Beach—Manukau Harbour

CAMERON *is waking up.* RICHARD *is rubbing some cream onto* ADELAIDE'*s ankle.*

CAMERON: Good God I'm as stiff as two petrified planks!

RICHARD: Sleep well did you, Carruthers?

CAMERON, *dryly*: Brilliantly, thank you. Why would one ever dream of sleeping on a mattress again! I really can't imagine! You?

RICHARD: Yes, like a log. Beautiful morning. I've been astir since five!

CAMERON: How very stalwart! Where's Kathryn?

ADELAIDE: She's gone to fetch water.

> RICHARD *looks at* ADELAIDE'*s ankle.*

RICHARD: Try flexing it again.

ADELAIDE: That feels better, Richard. You have healing hands.

RICHARD: It looks a sight better than it did last night.

CAMERON: You might not have to carry her after all, Swan!

> KATHRYN *comes back with water, which she gives to* ADELAIDE. *She gives the flint to* CAMERON.

CAMERON: Darling, where've you been?

ADELAIDE: You've been ages, Kathryn.

KATHRYN: I found the flint. You must've dropped it, Cammy.

CAMERON: Thank God! I can have a pipe at least! Small mercy in the wild!

ADELAIDE: What have you been doing?

KATHRYN: I talked to . . . to the woman with the little girl. She's agreed to lead us to the Traveller's Rest.

ADELAIDE: Oh, thank heavens!

CAMERON: I hardly think we should track our ploughshare with that feminine renegade!

KATHRYN: We have no other safe means out of here.

RICHARD: I thought she looked quite trustworthy.

CAMERON: Oh, come on man! Who *is* she for God's sake?

RICHARD: She looks like one of the Mokai Pakeha. White settlers who've been adopted by the natives.

CAMERON: Send her south with the Maoris, I'd say!

RICHARD: Good Lord, Carruthers! Why should the Maoris be sent packing! These are their homelands after all!

CAMERON: Oh please, not a bleeding heart liberal! Heaven knows, if the Maoris aren't brought to task, there'll be no enduring life in this colony for true Brits!

KATHRYN: How can you be so conservative, Cammy? On the one hand you're the rudest radical I know, on the other hand you're a stuffy prig! I do hope we don't have priggish children! I shall have to beat it out of them.

RICHARD: These Maori folk are human creatures, Carruthers, the work of the same omnipotent author as you and I! And equally under his care with the most polished European!

ADELAIDE: Shall we talk about something else! Like how we're going to travel ten miles on an empty stomach!

CAMERON: Yes, we'll probably die of starvation! We haven't eaten since lunch yesterday!

RICHARD: It's true. We've nothing but water. We'll be weak within an hour.

CAMERON: I vote we lose the mysterious lady of the missions and tackle the beach toute seule! Let's hope we meet up with our boys first! That woman will lead us up the giddy path! Mark my words, Swan.

There is a thud as something is thrown onto the ground. It is wrapped in flax. RICHARD *opens it.*

Richard: Breakfast! Wood pigeon. Very tasty actually.

He smiles facetiously at Cameron.

Richard: Still think she can't be trusted?

Pause.

Cameron: I need a wash.

Adelaide: So do I. Help me up, Cameron.

He does so.

Adelaide: Oh, Kathryn dear. You shall have to learn Viola's lines for me. This ankle really is quite sore.

Kathryn: I can't possibly learn all her speeches by tomorrow night!

Cameron: I wouldn't worry if I was you. We'll be lucky if we get back by next month!

Adelaide: But we simply must. We can't possibly let the Governor down.

Cameron: The man is managing a war, Adelaide! He's hardly likely to come and watch us strut and fret our hour upon the barrack floor! He's got more important scenes to direct.

Adelaide: The governor has always come to my performances!

Richard: I'll get some firewood. We'll feel better when we've had something to eat. We can do something with this pigeon at least.

Cameron *helps* Adelaide *off.*

Cameron: De-feather it by the time we return, Swan. My bird skinning skills are not what they used to be.

Adelaide: We can't possibly eat that thing?

Cameron: I'd sooner have a nasty piece of bread and dripping.

Kathryn *looks after them. She looks worried, puts her head in her hands for a moment, thinks.*

Richard: You look worried, Kathryn.

Kathryn *smiles.*

Kathryn: No, no . . . I'm fine. Really.

Richard *goes to his satchel and takes out a brown leather-bound copy of Shakespeare which he gives to* Kathryn.

RICHARD: I'll take you through these lines if you like.

> KATHRYN *takes the book and smiles at him.*

KATHRYN: You really are a nice man, Richard.

> RICHARD *laughs at himself.*

RICHARD: First class fool sometimes!

KATHRYN: I don't think so.

RICHARD: I'll fetch the firewood.

> *They smile in a sort of acknowledgment.*

KATHRYN: Thank you.

> KATHRYN *takes the book. She sits for a moment, frowning.*
> *Eventually she opens the book. Reads.* LUCY *comes on quietly*
> *and listens to* KATHRYN.

KATHRYN: 'Make me a willow cabin at your gate, And call upon
my soul within the house; Write loyal cantons of condemned
love and sing them loud even in the dead of night; Halloo
your name to the reverberate hills And make the babbling
gossip of the air cry out "Olivia!" O, You should not rest
between the elements of air and earth, but you should pity
me!'

> KATHRYN *sees* LUCY *and stops.*

KATHRYN: Come here . . . Come on . . .

> LUCY *stays where she is.* CHARLOTTE *enters unbeknown to*
> *either of them. She watches suspiciously.*

KATHRYN: Have you been spying on me?

> LUCY *doesn't respond.*

KATHRYN: Look here I'm only joking. You were probably enthralled
by Mr Shakespeare's words, weren't you? No, I don't expect
you've ever heard of him. Or Viola. Come on, come closer. I
shan't bite you.

> LUCY *doesn't move or say anything, just watches.* KATHRYN
> *picks up the book again keeping half an eye on* LUCY *as she*
> *reads.*

KATHRYN: 'Are *you* the Honourable lady of the house? Most radiant, exquisite and unmatchable beauty—I pray you tell me if you be the Honourable lady of the house . . .'

LUCY *creeps forward.*

KATHRYN: 'If I did love you in my Master's flame, with such a suff'ring, such a deadly life, in your denial I would find no sense; I would not understand it.'

LUCY *is transfixed by something shiny around* KATHRYN'*s neck. She puts a finger out to touch it.*

LUCY: He ataahua. (Beautiful.) He kohora tera. (Shiny.)

KATHRYN: You like the locket? Yes it's very pretty isn't it? It's not real. Just a piece of costume jewellery. But look here, it opens. See, it's shaped just like a heart. *(She opens it.)*

CHARLOTTE: Lucy! Haere mai ki konei! (Lucy! Come over here!)

KATHRYN: There's no need to be so rough with the child! She was only listening!

CHARLOTTE: Tryin' to find out wot crime I done? You're wasting yor time with her. She don't speak your tongue. *(To* LUCY.*)* Haere mai ki konei. Inaianei! (Come over here. Now!)

KATHRYN: Your ego really is rather inflated isn't it! I'm not in the slightest bit interested in your illicit past! And if I was, I wouldn't ask the child, I'd ask you! And as I know that won't get me anywhere, I won't waste my breath.

CHARLOTTE: Me hoki koe ki te whare. (Get back to the house.)

LUCY *shakes her head.*

KATHRYN: But feel free to stay and listen too if you like. You never know, you might learn a thing or two. Now where was I? 'I see you what you are, you are too proud, but if you were the devil, you are fair.'

CHARLOTTE: Nothin' I could learn from that lot!

KATHRYN: Oh, I expect there is. But in any case, I think Lucy was enjoying it. Weren't you, Lucy?

CHARLOTTE: I don't think so! An seein' as she don't have the birth and education of a gentlewoman, she's never likely to. *(To* LUCY.*)* Haere atu koe i a ia. (Get away from her.)

KATHRYN: 'Oh you should not rest between the elements of air
and earth but you should pity me.'
CHARLOTTE: I should not rest if you carry on with that toss. Haere
atu, Lucy! (Get away, Lucy!)
KATHRYN: You really are in a fidget over such an innocent thing as
a piece of poetry.
CHARLOTTE: I watched you trying to lure her.
KATHRYN: I hate to disabuse you, but the child sat with me of her
own accord.
CHARLOTTE: She's a green littl' loll. Thinks she can trust anyone.
KATHRYN: Not a virtue you share.

> CAMERON *comes back.*

CAMERON: What's going on? You're supposed to be learning your
lines, not conversing with these personages.

> LUCY *runs off.*

CHARLOTTE: I enjoyed your whisky. Got any more then?
CAMERON: I most certainly have not! And if I did, I wouldn't give
it. Seeing as you virtually thieved the last lot!
CHARLOTTE: No need to get nasty! I were only asking.
CAMERON: We can do without your questions, thank you. And
we don't require your help!
KATHRYN: We *do,* Cammy!
CAMERON: I'll be the best judge of that, Kathryn.
KATHRYN: It's too dangerous to attempt the journey alone.
CAMERON: Get on with your lines. I'll round up the others.

> *He goes.*

CHARLOTTE: He's a flash gent, in't he! Nice manners an' all!
KATHRYN: You're hardly in a position to judge my fiancé's manners.
Now if you don't mind, I have work to do.

> KATHRYN *reads the piece again.* CHARLOTTE *lights a pipe
> and drops to her haunches, listening.* KATHRYN *reads it
> beautifully.*

KATHRYN: 'Make me a willow cabin . . .'
CHARLOTTE: Loada toss that is!

KATHRYN *tries to ignore her.*

KATHRYN: 'Make me a willow cabin at your . . .'
CHARLOTTE: Waste of time, if you ask me.
KATHRYN: I wasn't asking you!
KATHRYN: However, if it wasn't for poetry and the written word, we would know very little about our past.
CHARLOTTE: Natives know their past. They don't need no books.
KATHRYN: No, but some of us like to read about it.
CHARLOTTE: Why?
KATHRYN: Well because . . . it helps us understand where we've come from.
CHARLOTTE: Why?
KATHRYN: Because . . . well because then we know why we are the way we are.
CHARLOTTE: Don't need no book to know why I am!
KATHRYN: You probably do. For example, where were you born?
CHARLOTTE: Well, your honour, I was present at my birth, but I cannot tell you the time or the place.
KATHRYN: Exactly!
CHARLOTTE: What's the good a' knowing that?

CHARLOTTE *gets out a pipe.*

KATHRYN: You imagine this country in a hundred and fifty years from now. Imagine if we don't write about it? There'll be no record of the fighting on the Great South Road. No record of travellers like you or I. Unless some poet or painter leaves a glimpse of a time gone by, no one will ever know what happened. People will just forget.

Pause. CHARLOTTE *thinks for a moment.*

CHARLOTTE: You wanna know my crime?

KATHRYN *looks at her, surprised.*

KATHRYN: I have some minor curiosity, yes.
CHARLOTTE: I fobbed four guineas, a silver coin, an' an 'alf-crown.
KATHRYN: Is that all?
CHARLOTTE: No, your honour I lie, there were also one silk hanksnif.

Pause.

KATHRYN: Then you're not a murderess?

CHARLOTTE *scoffs.*

CHARLOTTE: Ain't no angel neither.

KATHRYN: I hadn't mistaken you for one.

Silence.

CHARLOTTE: Nearly I got away wi' it. But I got nibbed by a crusher on the beat. Sentenced to seven years across the herring pond.

Silence.

KATHRYN: And what about the scoundrels with whom you beat the captain?

CHARLOTTE: Couple of good cobbers they were. We clubbed together for a while, we three, an' we saw nothin' wrong with that.

KATHRYN: Clubbed together?

CHARLOTTE: Three in a bunk.

KATHRYN: Oh. You mean . . . a *ménage à trois*?

CHARLOTTE: Wot's that?

KATHRYN: French, for a threesome.

CHARLOTTE: Could say that.

KATHRYN *is a little appalled.*

KATHRYN: Oh how . . . how truly modern.

CHARLOTTE: Don't know 'bout that.

KATHRYN: I'm a freethinker, you know.

CHARLOTTE: Are you an' all?

Pause.

KATHRYN: Was he the father of the little one?

CHARLOTTE: Not likely, her father was the turnkey at the Parramatta Prison. Spent five years of me precious youth there. Then they shipped us down to the worst colony in the country. She were only a babe in arms when we took that tug.

KATHRYN: You stole an entire ship! You're not entirely innocent! That's a little bit bigger than a handkerchief!

CHARLOTTE: Only a little bit bigger, Miss.

KATHRYN: *And* they say you raided other ships along the way! That's common piracy!

CHARLOTTE: Had to have supplies, din't we?

> *Pause.*

KATHRYN: And your colleagues? What happened to them?

CHARLOTTE: They catched Ben soon as we landed here. Shipped him back to London.

KATHRYN: And . . . and the woman?

CHARLOTTE: Died.

KATHRYN: Oh.

> KATHRYN *senses there is a sadness there and is almost awkward. Pause.*

KATHRYN: Well I . . . I think the English judiciary is an ass. Transporting people for little more than a penny loaf or a few shillings.

> *Silence.* CHARLOTTE *looks away into the middle distance.*

CHARLOTTE: Thought I found heaven when we saw them Bay of Islands. No need for stealin' there. Chief give us a little hut on the beach. When the whale ships comes in, you get anything you like. Salt beef, pork, 'bacco. Plenty a' grog shops then, plenty a' good ale. An' every so often you gets a lad like me, comes ashore, escaping from the cat-o'-nine-tails.

KATHRYN: Then why didn't you stay?

> CHARLOTTE *lights a pipe.*

CHARLOTTE: Gov' cut all the trade see. With them whalers. So the fightin' started. Time ta move on. We tried living 'mongst the white folk, but we 'ad nothin' in common. So we comes back to the Maori. Treat us like their own, see.

> *Pause.*

KATHRYN: Well you're no saint, that's for sure. But I . . . I don't know any woman who has done such . . . such bold things.

CHARLOTTE: Nothin' to it!

KATHRYN: I doubt that.

CHARLOTTE: I just puts one foot in front of the other. Just like you do, Miss.

KATHRYN: No. Not just like I do . . .

KATHRYN looks a little rueful and turns her gaze away. CHARLOTTE scrutinises her then takes out her pipe, packs it with tobacco. They sit in silence for a bit.

CHARLOTTE: You're very fortful, Miss.

KATHRYN: Am I?

CHARLOTTE: What you thinkin' an' all?

KATHRYN looks into the middle distance.

KATHRYN: That I should like to run wild in a wood forever.

Pause. CHARLOTTE looks into the middle distance.

CHARLOTTE: I'd rather die than be locked up again.

KATHRYN: But you're free now . . . Free to do as you please.

CHARLOTTE: Aye. I am an' all.

There is a moment of silence. CHARLOTTE breaks it.

CHARLOTTE: It's gonna rain. I can feel it.

CHARLOTTE relights her pipe.

KATHRYN: Yes, well, I really must get back to my work!

CHARLOTTE: Don't mind me, Miss. 'Eard a lotta rubbish in my time.

KATHRYN: Then I invite you to leave! *(Picks up book, slightly peeved.)* 'I see you what you are, you are too proud, but . . .'

CHARLOTTE, *picks up the line she's heard earlier*: '. . . but if you were the devil, you are fair.'

KATHRYN takes a moment to register, then looks at her amused and nonplussed.

KATHRYN: You memorised that? You have extraordinary recall.

CHARLOTTE, *grins*: Trick a' the trade you might say. Acquir'd it outta necessity.

KATHRYN positions herself once more to learn the lines.

KATHRYN: No doubt for ill purposes. *(Returns to book.)*

CHARLOTTE: Ooh, I wouldn't say that, Miss.

KATHRYN: 'Make me a willow cabin at your gate . . .'

> CHARLOTTE *lights a pipe and settles back to listen to her.*
> KATHRYN *continues* sotto voce *under the following. On the
> other side of the stage,* CAMERON *and* ADELAIDE *are washing
> with a damp handkerchief.*

CAMERON: That man's a first class idiot! I was a fool to be led into
this.

ADELAIDE: It was Kathryn insisted that we come!

CAMERON: Oh, do stop blaming Kathryn!

ADELAIDE: Oh, Cammy, I'm frightened.

> *He softens, puts his arms around her.*

CAMERON: Come here. It will be alright. Trust me. I shall have us
back at the barracks by nightfall.

> *Chanting.*

ADELAIDE: Those sounds are getting closer.

CAMERON: Yes, we'll get back on the road as soon as possible.

ADELAIDE: But surely we can't risk it. She said we'd be . . .

CAMERON: She was trying to unnerve us. Now I suggest we round
up the others and . . .

> CAMERON *sees something.*

ADELAIDE, *stricken*: What is it?

CAMERON, *whispers*: Don't make a sound.

> *The drums grow louder, menacing. On the other side of the
> stage the scene between* KATHRYN *and* CHARLOTTE
> *continues.*

KATHRYN: '. . . you should not rest between the elements of air
and earth but you should pity me.'

CHARLOTTE: D'you like bein' on the stage an' all?

KATHRYN: Yes . . . yes, of course I do.

CHARLOTTE: Bit like my line a' work, innit?

> KATHRYN *laughs despite herself.*

KATHRYN: Yes. Except that *you* don't get the applause.

CHARLOTTE: Rotten tomatas more like!

KATHRYN, *smiles.* That's true I suppose.

CHARLOTTE: You're very pretty when you smile.

> KATHRYN *is clearly embarrassed.*

KATHRYN: You are interrupting my work.

CHARLOTTE: A dimber mort you is.

KATHRYN: A what?

CHARLOTTE: Beautiful. It means beautiful.

> *Pause.* KATHRYN *is embarrassed and returns to her book.* CAMERON *rushes back, in a panic.*

CAMERON: Kathryn darling! Thank God you're alright! There's a party of natives at the edge of the bush! They didn't see us, thank God!

KATHRYN: We must leave here immediately.

CHARLOTTE: Better follow me!

CAMERON: I refuse to be led by this vagabond!

CHARLOTTE: Listen prick! If you wanna end up in the soup, stay here! Otherwise shut yor bone box an' follow me!

CAMERON: Charming.

KATHRYN: I suggest we do what she says!

Scene 9: Beach

Waves crashing. Rain. ADELAIDE *limps on, wet, bedraggled, propped up by* RICHARD, *and limping with a stick for extra support.* RICHARD *has his coat around her.* CAMERON *is equally miserable, following several steps behind.*

ADELAIDE: Richard, I can't go much further.

RICHARD: Stop here a moment and rest.

CAMERON: Don't let's lose the others for Chrissake!

RICHARD: Can't you see she's in no state! Even the child can't keep up.

CAMERON: Whose fault is that!

RICHARD: Make yourself useful, Carruthers! Run on ahead and tell them we've stopped!

CAMERON: Run on ahead! What do you think I am, the stagehand? I'm not going near that gorgon! Every time I open my mouth she growls like a rabid dog!

RICHARD: I can't say I blame her.

CAMERON: I'm rather tiring of your bodacious remarks, boy!

RICHARD: Don't call me boy!

CAMERON: What shall I call you then? A talent-free pussy?

ADELAIDE: Oh, for God's sake stop it! This nightmare is wretched enough without you two being disagreeable!

RICHARD: Yes, why sink to the lowest common denominator? I'll go on ahead myself. You can't walk any longer. Look after her, Carruthers.

He dashes off.

ADELAIDE: Can you at least *try* and possess yourself!

CAMERON: He's a tedious thing! And I don't know what you see in him!

ADELAIDE: He's kind.

CAMERON: Unlike me.

ADELAIDE: Yes, unlike you!

CAMERON: And you fancy him rotten!

ADELAIDE: You're jealous.

CAMERON: He's a dull, earnest little man and he'll bore you dilly in bed!

ADELAIDE: He has very sexy eyes.

CAMERON: Sexy! They're pathetic little pissholes in the snow! I don't know what's sexy about them!

ADELAIDE: You *are* jealous! Go on admit it!

CAMERON: Yes, I am jealous! Why shouldn't I be?

ADELAIDE: Do I get jealous of your fiancée?

CAMERON *doesn't answer.*

CAMERON: Let's not talk about that!

ADELAIDE: *Do* I?

CAMERON: Can we change the subject please!

ADELAIDE: I was merely making the point that *I* am extremely accepting of your amours.

CAMERON: Kathryn is an absolute angel.

ADELAIDE: And that's what you want isn't it.

ADELAIDE *says this more as a statement than a question. She shivers.* CAMERON *takes his scarf off and puts it around her.*

CAMERON: Here. Take this. You'll catch your death.

Pause.

ADELAIDE: Oh, Cammy, we will be alright won't we?

He puts his arm around her and talks in a genuinely caring way.

CAMERON: Of course we will! We've done a damn sight worse than this! We've survived more than a swollen ankle and a few silly little skirmishes!
ADELAIDE: Yes, we have . . . haven't we.

Pause.

CAMERON: Remember that night in Birmingham? The night we slept in the barn with no hay? And that blighter of a cook coming at us with his mad cow?

ADELAIDE *laughs remembering.*

ADELAIDE: Oh yes, I thought we'd be murdered in our beds that night!
CAMERON: He took a shine to you. Can't say he liked me much!
ADELAIDE: No, and remember that time we got locked in the basement at the Adelphi!
CAMERON: Never thought we'd get out that night! Couldn't you just see the headlines! Skeletal remains of thespians found in theatrical peat bog! And what about that leading nutter of yours in Derry? Wanted to kill us both that night. Remember? That look on his face when he caught us in the wings? And I had to go onstage and fight the bastard! I parried for dear life *that* night! I still bear the grim reminder of his wrath!

He rubs and flexes his hand, where he has a scar. ADELAIDE *laughs.*

ADELAIDE: Oh yes, he was capable.
CAMERON: We survived all that, didn't we!
ADELAIDE: Yes, we did.

Cameron: And you were beautiful that night. You were radiant
. . . Remember?

> Adelaide *smiles in a reminiscent way, nods. Pause, as they
> remember.* Cameron *tightens his arms around her.*

Adelaide: I sometimes wonder why we do it. Don't you? God
knows it's not for the merciless remuneration.

> *His voice is very gentle with her.*

Cameron: We do it because it lights up people's lives. Think of
the people who might never have laughed last night.
Adelaide: You're right . . . yes, you are right.
Cameron: And we do it because there's bugger all else we *can* do.
Adelaide: So we will be alright then?
Cameron: Of course we will. We'll be out of here in no time.
Adelaide: I'm fearful it's going to pour down.
Cameron: Rubbish! We won't let it.

> Cameron *pulls out a tin whistle and plays a line of 'Hey
> Ho the Wind and the Rain!'* Adelaide *laughs.* Lucy *emerges
> from the edge of the trees and looks at them.* Richard *returns,
> panting.*

Richard: There's no sign of them. They galloped on ahead!
Cameron: Oh, that's all we need!
Adelaide: But that's dreadful.
Richard: We need to hurry before this weather sets in.
Adelaide: Yes, we must make the performance, but I simply can't
walk any faster.
Richard: There's some shelter just up ahead. We'll make a litter
out of coats and poles. Find another pole, Carruthers.

> Cameron *goes over to the edge of the trees where the child
> has appeared. Lightning. In the flash of lightning, it is as if*
> Cameron *and* Lucy *are suddenly frozen in an eerie
> silhouette. They look at each other.* Cameron *speaks to the
> child in a quiet and gentle tone, as if transfixed by her other-
> worldliness.*

Cameron: Strange little thing aren't you . . .

He takes the tin whistle out of his coat and hands it to her.
LUCY *takes it, and at that moment there is the haunting
sounds of a tin whistle. Thunderclap.*

RICHARD: Hurry up! It's about to bucket down.
CAMERON: Oh great. Now we really are poked!

Scene 10: Beach

CHARLOTTE *is walking at a furious pace.* KATHRYN *is attempting to
keep up.*

KATHRYN: You're deliberately rushing on ahead! You know very
well one of our party is having trouble walking.
CHARLOTTE: I said I'd lead you outta here, not 'ave a bleedin'
picnic on the way! Them that falls by the wayside, is not
worth waitin' for!
KATHRYN: Are you always this cold and callous?

CHARLOTTE *turns on her.*

CHARLOTTE: I'm risking my neck for the likes of you!
KATHRYN: And you're getting well remunerated!
CHARLOTTE: The sooner I'm rid a' you the better!
KATHRYN: If you think trying to separate me from the others is
going to get you what you want, you're sadly mistaken. My
fiancé holds all the money.

CHARLOTTE *grabs her violently by the hair.*

KATHRYN: You'd never get away with it! They'll hang you for it in
the end!
CHARLOTTE: Listen Lady! I coulda done you twenty times by now!
If I wanted to kill you I wouldn't a' ' barked on this bleedin'
little beach walk would I! Maoris have always trusted me! It's
yor lot wot are shuntin' them down the river! If they see me
with the likes of you, I'll have a thing to answer!
KATHRYN: I'll thank you to let go of me!
CHARLOTTE: I give the orders here, Miss! So just shut it!

Kathryn *scoffs.*

Kathryn: If you think you can intimidate me with violent, troublesome threats, you're quite mistaken! You truly are pathetic! And if you weren't so unpleasant, I'd pity you!
Charlotte: Pity me! That's a laugh. I'm happy with my lot! An' the way I see it, it's the other way round. It's me wot should pity you!

Kathryn *is incredulous.*

Kathryn: Oh, you truly are conceited! Why on earth you should pity me, I really can't imagine!
Charlotte: I see things, don't I?
Kathryn: I have never met anyone so extraordinarily arrogant! Whatever it is that you think you see, you've got it entirely wrong! You're no seer that's for sure!
Charlotte: I sense things about people.
Kathryn: Oh really? Do you really? Well it hardly requires psychic power to see I'm deeply distressed by our current plight. Now I asked you to *let go* of me!
Charlotte: I'll let go of you if you stop your cant and don't start it again till we get there.
Kathryn: I have no intention of 'stopping my cant'! Why should I? I have a perfect right to my opinions just as you do!
Charlotte: No wonder your future hubby finds you difficult!
Kathryn: My fiancé does *not* find me difficult. It's you that's difficult and you're projecting that entirely onto me!
Charlotte: Your voker gives me an 'eadache! You got enough tongue for two sets a' teeth.
Kathryn: You are the most chauvinistic woman I have ever met. You're worse than a man! Do you realise that? And if you could see how unfeminine you look in those breeches! Really. No man would ever look twice at you . . .

Charlotte, *who still has* Kathryn *by the hair, pulls her to her and kisses her violently on the mouth. When she lets go, she has an arrogant smirk on her face.* Kathryn *is shocked to her core.* Kathryn*'s voice is low with rage.*

Kathryn: How dare you!

CHARLOTTE *grins.*

CHARLOTTE: Got anything else to say then, have we?

Thunderclap. Blackout.

Scene 11: The Traveller's Rest Inn

Sound of pouring rain. ADELAIDE *and* RICHARD *hobble in, in a bad state. They are totally wet and dishevelled.* RICHARD *carries his tripod and satchel and assists* ADELAIDE *at the same time.*

ADELAIDE: Oh thank God.

RICHARD, *calls*: Anybody here?

ADELAIDE: Thank God we made it!

RICHARD: You were very brave with that ankle!

ADELAIDE: You've been wonderful, Richard. A tower of strength. I never thought we'd make it.

RICHARD: It was fortunate the child knew the way.

> WALLY, *a Scotsman, and the proprietor of the hotel, enters. He's a bit of a drinker.*

WALLY: Well I'll be buggered! You really are a bedraggled lot! Wallace Campbell, call me Wally. How on earth you got past the guns and the whistles I'll never know! But you're welcome! Welcome at the Traveller's Rest!

ADELAIDE: Thank you. Thank you.

RICHARD: Our colleagues are right behind us! Do you have room for one night?

WALLY: There's always room at the Inn!

ADELAIDE: Oh thank you, Mr Campbell, it really has been a toilsome day.

RICHARD: I've never been so glad to see a pub in my life!

WALLY: We've had a deal of excitement ourselves. We've been in a state of defence all day. The bush was lit up with a terrific volley. We've had Forest Rangers here, cutting rifle slits in the walls.

ADELAIDE: We *are* safe then?

WALLY: Ooh yes, couldn't be safer! The Rangers have set up their headquarters here!

ADELAIDE: Oh thank God!

WALLY: You've got Ring's Redoubt down the road. That's garrisoned by the 18th Royal Irish Regiment. You'd have passed them on the way.

RICHARD: We came up through the forest, from the beach.

WALLY: Then you're lucky you're still alive! That forest is riddled with savages! They infest the bush like wild animals.

ADELAIDE: Oh, I feel faint.

WALLY: Down the road still further, you've got the Presbyterian church and that's been loopholed for rifle-fire. Visibly transformed you might say, from a bulwark of faith to a bulwark of bullet power!

ADELAIDE: Oh how comforting.

RICHARD: Do you think we might get back to Auckland tomorrow?

ADELAIDE: We're due to perform at the Albert Barracks.

WALLY: Performers! Oh aye. Supply wagon goes back in the morning. Get you to the steamer what'll take you to Onehunga. Now, medicinal whiskys?

ADELAIDE: Thank you. How very kind.

He goes. ADELAIDE *looks at* RICHARD *in relief.*

ADELAIDE: I must look awful.

RICHARD: You look radiant, even when beaten by gale force winds!

ADELAIDE: You flatter me.

RICHARD: No, not at all. Your husband must tell you so often.

ADELAIDE: I'm afraid not. He's rather occupied with his circus.

RICHARD: Surely he must sing your praises to the four winds!

ADELAIDE: More likely to the four mistresses.

RICHARD: Oh. I see.

ADELAIDE: My husband has not sung my praises for a long time, Richard. He rather sings to the intolerable Madame Tournear, a circus artiste of dubious talents!

RICHARD: Oh, Adelaide, I see . . . I did wonder.

ADELAIDE: She did me a service in fact. No, it was my children that she . . . corrupted from me.

RICHARD: Oh, Adelaide, how awful . . .

ADELAIDE: But that's another life now, Richard. The past is another
country.

RICHARD: Yes. I understand. More than you realise.

ADELAIDE *nods. Pause.*

RICHARD: But this husband of yours, he must've been a blackguard
of the highest order!

ADELAIDE: I'm no innocent, Richard.

RICHARD: You're a sophisticated woman. I'd be blind not to see
that.

ADELAIDE: I have had many men.

RICHARD: I see.

ADELAIDE: But I have never yet known *the* man . . . that in my
mind, I have always wanted to know . . .

RICHARD: Then I hope one day you will, Mrs Foley . . .

ADELAIDE: I hope so too, Mr Swan . . .

KATHRYN *and* CAMERON *enter.*

KATHRYN: Cameron, you really are impossible!

CAMERON: That harridan of a woman deliberately rushed on ahead.

KATHRYN: Yes, but she did *not* deliberately push you off the rocks!
Although *I* would've done so, had you been so inconsiderately
rude towards *me!*

CAMERON: I do think you're being just a little bit harsh!

KATHRYN: Your string of abuse was unmanly.

CAMERON: She was as belligerent as a rabid banshee towards *me!*
When she wasn't masticating wrathful words, she was trying
to do me an injury! What did I *say* for God's sake? What did
I do *wrong?*

KATHRYN: Dear sweet, unjust, generous, impulsive, pig-headed
Cameron! Never have I known such conflicting qualities in
a man! That someone who can play the underdog to
perfection onstage, can in real life be so unforgiving and so
cruelly unkind to someone who is so clearly disadvantaged
in life!

CAMERON: Disadvantaged! She's not in the least disadvantaged!
She roams the country, with complete immunity from the
Maori! She's as arrogant as any pig of a man I've come across,
and she looks as if she's never lacked a decent meal in her

life! Why you're suddenly defending her I don't know!

KATHRYN: I am not defending her! She appals me! But if the poorer classes get treated like animals, they behave like animals. It's obvious just looking at her physique, she's lived a hard life!

CAMERON: I'm not interested in the unlovely properties of her physique. Or lack of one. I just want you to be kind to me. You've been a perfect piglet and you know it!

Pause. KATHRYN *sighs.*

KATHRYN: Yes, I'm sorry. It's been a strain, that's all.

He puts his arms around her and kisses her forehead.

CAMERON: Of course it has. That's better. That's my girl.

KATHRYN *sighs as* WALLY *comes back with a tray of whisky.*

CAMERON: Oh jolly good, old chap! Jolly good timing!

CAMERON *takes a glass.*

CAMERON: Just what the doctor ordered!

WALLY: We've just heard from the friendly Maoris that some settlers were attacked and murdered in Kerikeri last night. A couple of them were harmless old people.

CAMERON: Good God! They're complete savages!

WALLY: Those Kingites are killers alright! They've been attacking convoys on the road. Thank God the Brits mowed thirty of them down last week!

KATHRYN: Then presumably the Brits are killers as well!

WALLY: They're just doing their job, Miss. If the savages won't leave peacefully, we can't sit supinely by, and wait for them to carry war into Auckland.

CAMERON: Certainly not!

WALLY: They've been permitted to roam about with impunity. And now look what's happening! They're inflicting the most cruel barbarities on peaceable settlers and tomahawking our neighbours!

KATHRYN *mutters underneath her breath.*

KATHRYN: Oh, I cannot abide this civil stupidity!

She starts to storm out.

CAMERON: Kathryn, where are you going?
KATHRYN: To the outhouse!

> WALLY *calls out after her.*

WALLY: Round to the right, Miss.
CAMERON: Be careful, Kathryn! For God's sake be careful!

> WALLY *holds out his hand to* CAMERON.

WALLY: Wallace Campbell. Call me Wally! Another drop? It quells the stomach.

> CAMERON *shakes his hand and holds his glass out.* WALLY *refills it.*

CAMERON: I need a little quelling, after following our unfortunate guide from the Mission station.
WALLY: Mission station? What Mission station?
CAMERON: The one in Papakura.
WALLY: Ooh, there's no Mission station in Papakura. Oh no.
CAMERON: Well there is, I'm sure.
WALLY: No, I know the village well. I've lived here a long time. Ever since I came back from the California gold rush.

> CAMERON *downs his drink quickly.*

CAMERON: Excuse me!

> CAMERON *rushes out. There is a pause as the others watch him go.*

ADELAIDE: Do you think we might be shown to our rooms?
RICHARD: And could I trouble you for some running water? I should like to develop some photographic plates.
WALLY: Follow me. Your wish is my command!

> *They exit.*

Scene 12: Outside The Traveller's Rest Inn

KATHRYN *comes outside, wrapping her shawl around her.* CHARLOTTE *comes up behind her, very threateningly.*

CHARLOTTE: Thought you tried to do a runner!

KATHRYN: I could hardly say 'excuse me while I pop out and give away my papers' now could I?

CHARLOTTE: Where's the money?

KATHRYN: My fiancé keeps it. You'll have to wait till morning. I'll get it when he's asleep.

CHARLOTTE: How do I know you won't blow the gaff on me?

KATHRYN: Very trusting I must say!

CHARLOTTE: I kept my end of the lay.

> KATHRYN *gives her the passport.*

KATHRYN: Yes, you did. We leave for the Albert Barracks at dawn. Here, take the papers as good faith.

> CHARLOTTE *takes them.*

CHARLOTTE: How do I know this ain't a trap?

KATHRYN: Your problem is you've never been able to trust anyone in your life. Not everyone is a dishonest rogue.

> *Pause.* CHARLOTTE *nods, convinced.*

CHARLOTTE: You got an honest set a' lamps.

> KATHRYN *smiles at the colourful description of her eyes.*

KATHRYN: Thank you.

> *Pause.*

KATHRYN: I'll meet you here at sunrise.

> *Pause.*

CHARLOTTE: You gimme your word then?

> KATHRYN *looks at her sincerely.*

KATHRYN: I give you my word.

CHARLOTTE *leaves.* KATHRYN *sees* LUCY, *hovering in the shadows looking at her.*

KATHRYN: Off you go Lucy . . . Go on . . . Off you go. Shoo!

LUCY *just stands there for a moment then leaves.* KATHRYN *stands there for a long moment, looking into the night. She looks troubled. At a loss. She wraps her coat around her and hugs herself.*

Scene 13: Richard Swan's Hotel Bedroom

RICHARD *has his 'photographic tent' set up on its tripod. He is under a black cloth, which covers his upper half. There is a bucket of water on the floor and a tin case, which contains his portable travelling darkroom equipment. On a chair beside him are some glass wet plates.*

He emerges from under the tent, and looks at the plate he's just developed. He looks confused. He recognises it as Charlotte, but is bemused as to what she's holding—an object that looks like a pistol. He holds it up to the light and looks completely disbelieving. He is still mulling over it when ADELAIDE *comes in. She wears a dressing gown and carries her clothes over her arm.*

ADELAIDE: Good morning, Richard.

RICHARD *doesn't look at her, but is still studying the plate.*

RICHARD: Adelaide, good morning! I've just developed this curious
    plate . . . Been at it all night actually . . .
ADELAIDE: Richard, I hate to incommode you but . . .
RICHARD: There's something peculiar about this . . .
ADELAIDE: . . . but I had just finished my ablutions when to my
    chagrin, I find I have no dry towels left at all. I wondered if
    I might trouble you for one?
RICHARD: Yes, yes, of course.
ADELAIDE: Thank you, Richard.
RICHARD: This plate has completely bamboozled me! It's got to be
    one that Kathryn took of our mysterious guide. But the funny
    thing is it looks as if she's holding a . . .

RICHARD *looks at* ADELAIDE *for the first time. She is standing very seductively, undoing her dressing gown. He is quite stopped in his tracks.*

RICHARD: Oh, you do look beautiful . . .

ADELAIDE *'s voice is low and sensuous.*

ADELAIDE: I'm very wet . . .

RICHARD *catches his breath. Swallows.*

RICHARD: There's . . . there's a towel just over there . . . just on that chair . . .

ADELAIDE: I shall catch my death if I don't dry myself.

RICHARD: Yes, yes of course you must! I'll wait outside!

ADELAIDE: No, Richard! You are a gentleman I'm sure!

RICHARD: . . . I'll develop another plate!

He puts his head back under the black cloth and talks from underneath it. ADELAIDE *undoes her gown and picks up the towel as he speaks to her.*

RICHARD: You know, it's a curious thing . . . That plate I developed before. I don't know whether it's a trick of the lens or what. It surely was a peculiar light that day we explored the hinterland. But it does look for all the world as if our woman companion was pointing a . . .

ADELAIDE *interrupts him.*

ADELAIDE: Richard! I wonder if I could trouble you for another towel. This one really is wet also.

RICHARD: Oh, yes, yes of course. I've been using it for the developing.

ADELAIDE *is facing* RICHARD, *her dressing gown slipped open.*

RICHARD: I mean, it can't possibly be so, of course, but in my limited knowledge, it really does look as if she's holding a . . .

RICHARD *comes out from under the black cloth and looks at* ADELAIDE. *He stops mid sentence.*

RICHARD: Oh, you are lovely . . .

He swallows.

RICHARD: Your . . . your breasts are so . . . so . . .

ADELAIDE *helps him out.*

ADELAIDE: So in need of rubbing dry.

He goes over to her, unable to keep his eyes off her breasts. He puts both hands out slowly and barely touches them. He finally does so. His touch is delicate.

RICHARD: Oh, Adelaide. Adelaide. Oh I am in heaven . . . They are . . . exquisite . . . exquisite . . .

He drops to his knees. Running his hands down her body. And then suddenly they both abandon themselves. CAMERON *enters.*

CAMERON, *entering:* Have you seen Kathryn? I woke up and she wasn't there!

CAMERON *sees them.*

CAMERON: Oh don't mind me! Seen it all before.

ADELAIDE: Richard was just massaging my sore ankle.

CAMERON: Yes, of course he was.

RICHARD: I was indeed . . .

They are both dishevelled and move to the other side of the camera and make a pretence of looking at the ankle. They're so busy with it that they take no notice of CAMERON *picking up and looking at the photographic plates as he talks.*

CAMERON: Carry on with your guilty commerce. I'm concerned about Kathryn. She's been peculiar ever since we met that mad woman from the mission, or non-mission as the case may be. It's clear she was lying through her unfortunate teeth . . .

He has found the plate of CHARLOTTE *and looks at it closely, holding it up to the light. He puts on his glasses and studies it closer. There's no doubt in his mind.*

CAMERON: Good God . . .

He takes the plate with him and rushes out.

Scene 14: Outside The Traveller's Rest Inn

KATHRYN *is standing outside, looking into the dawn light, waiting for* CHARLOTTE *to turn up. She appears out of the shadows.*

CHARLOTTE: You got the guineas then?

KATHRYN: I said I'd keep my word. And I've done so.

KATHRYN *is about to get them out of her pocket.*

CAMERON, *off*: Kathryn.

CHARLOTTE, *looking round in a panic*: You gone an' done me to the crushers!

KATHRYN: No!

CAMERON, *off*: Kathryn!

CHARLOTTE: Should never a' trusted you!

KATHRYN: But wait, I . . .

CAMERON *comes rushing out,* KATHRYN *looks alarmed.*

KATHRYN: Cameron! What're you doing here?

CAMERON: I might ask the same of you!

KATHRYN: I couldn't sleep! I . . . I thought I'd watch the sunrise.

CAMERON: You knew who she was didn't you?

KATHRYN: What are you talking about?

CAMERON: You know very well what I'm talking about! You knew who she was!

KATHRYN: You're talking in riddles.

CAMERON: You took the damn portrait of her! God! I should've realised! She's been in all the newspapers.

Pause.

CAMERON: Why didn't you tell me!

Pause.

KATHRYN: I couldn't risk it.

CAMERON: So you imperilled our lives?

KATHRYN: I was trying to protect us.

CAMERON: You might've told us after she scampered! You had ample opportunity!

KATHRYN: I was frightened . . .

Pause.

CAMERON: Oh, my poor darling. Of course you were. You must've been petrified. Having a pistol trained on you at close range.

CAMERON *puts his arms around her.*

CAMERON: You really were very brave, darling. God this is an odious place. The sooner we get back to England the better. Why didn't you tell me?

KATHRYN: You were always so . . . so mindful of Adelaide . . . Anyone would think you were engaged to *her*, not me.

CAMERON: Don't be ridiculous. Adelaide is not my type!

KATHRYN: Promise?

CAMERON: Oh, Katie, is that what's been bothering you?

KATHRYN: Yes . . . yes probably it is . . .

Pause.

CAMERON: Oh, darling, are you morose?

KATHRYN: A little muddled, that's all.

CAMERON: No wonder. Come on. You should eat something. Come inside now.

KATHRYN: I can't! I mean . . . I can't eat . . . It's too early.

CAMERON: Then come and rest before the coach leaves. You'll need a mind for learning Adelaide's lines.

KATHRYN: Why are you so unkind to Mr Swan?

CAMERON: Oh don't let's talk about him. *You* are my angel and you're safe now.

He kisses her cheek.

KATHRYN: Cammy, I can't possibly learn Adelaide's speeches by tonight. It really is impossible.

CAMERON: Rubbish! Nothing is impossible! First you knock the poor impossibilities down, second you kick them where they lie, and third you walk over their prostrate bodies!

KATHRYN *laughs despite herself.*

KATHRYN: Oh, Cammy. I do love you.

CAMERON: There now! That's better! Come on.

KATHRYN *looks around for* CHARLOTTE, *wondering what to do.* CAMERON *leads her off.*

CAMERON: Thank God that woman's buggered off!

Scene 15: Albert Barracks—Auckland

CAPTAIN PETERS *from the Albert Barracks leads* ADELAIDE *into the dressing room of the military theatre. He carries two of the troupe's cases.* KATHRYN *and* CAMERON *follow.*

CAPTAIN PETERS: Welcome to the Albert Barracks, Mrs Foley. It's a great honour to have such a famous lady in our midst.

ADELAIDE, *smiling sweetly:* Why thank you, Captain.

CAPTAIN PETERS, *giving* ADELAIDE *his arm:* We certainly need some entertainment, Ma'am. There's been great anxiety here in the capital of Auckland. You were very lucky to get past the Maori revenge parties. They're a slippery lot! They assemble in armed bands and skirmish from tree to tree keeping up a hot fire! Now, this is the dressing room. It's a bit makeshift I'm afraid.

He puts the cases down.

ADELAIDE: It'll do nicely, Captain.

CAPTAIN PETERS: You'll have an appreciative audience. The Governor's called up all unmarried men and we have the first draft of 400 citizen recruits here tonight. A full house of eager young bucks. Barely weaned off their mother's milk. They're looking forward to some good, wholesome comicalities!

ADELAIDE: Then we shall bring smiles to their faces.

CAPTAIN PETERS: I am told you enact Shakespeare superbly.

ADELAIDE, *visibly flattered, flirting:* I aim to please, Captain.

CAPTAIN PETERS: Might I get you anything, Mrs Foley?

CAMERON: Tumbler of whisky old man. Warm the vocal cords!

KATHRYN: Cameron, please!

CAPTAIN PETERS: Done!

CAMERON: Get the voice going, Katie! You know how it is. Me, me, me! Moo, mo, more, mar, may, me . . .

KATHRYN *looks at him despairingly.*

CAPTAIN PETERS: I look forward to your performance, Ma'am.
ADELAIDE: Then I shall not disappoint.

CAPTAIN PETERS *exits.*

ADELAIDE: Kathryn darling, I think I *can* perform Viola after all!
KATHRYN: But I have taken great pains to learn Viola!
ADELAIDE: I really do feel much revived.
CAMERON: Just popping out for a pipe!
ADELAIDE: Cameron. We're about to go on!
CAMERON: Quick puff, darling. Back by the time you've sung your
aria.

Applause as ADELAIDE *enters.* KATHRYN *is thoroughly
annoyed.*

Scene 16: Outside Albert Barracks

*Night. The others remain onstage in the background. It is an indoor/
outdoor scene, with split realities, that intersect with each other. It is
dark on the side of the stage and a sliver of light falls from a nearby
door. The distant sound of applause as* ADELAIDE *goes onstage. She
starts singing an aria.* CAMERON *steps outside with his tumbler of
whisky. He lights a pipe.* CHARLOTTE *and* LUCY *approach the barracks.*
LUCY *is holding some ragged belongings.* CHARLOTTE *is dressed in
her shirtsleeves. She stops and listens. She's tense, jumpy, and looks
behind her.* CAMERON *is busy swigging his whisky, he gargles, swills it
around his throat, swallows. He sees* CHARLOTTE *and steps back into
the shadows. She hasn't seen him.* CHARLOTTE *moves closer to the
stage door and listens.* CAMERON *comes up behind* CHARLOTTE. *And
speaks in a quiet voice.*

CAMERON: 'Ill met by moonlight', *Charlotte Badger.*

CHARLOTTE *freezes.*

CAMERON: That *is* your name, isn't it?
CHARLOTTE: Thought I seen the last of your ugly mug!
CAMERON: Unfortunately not. What do you want?

CHARLOTTE: I wanna word wi' yor fiancée.

CAMERON: I should think you want a word with the local police.

CHARLOTTE: Don't wanna raise no dust.

> *They stand like two dogs, each waiting for the other to make a move before they pounce. Applause from inside.* ADELAIDE *comes off and starts changing into Viola's costume. Onstage,* RICHARD *is playing Malvolio to* KATHRYN's *Olivia. It is interspersed with* CAMERON *and* CHARLOTTE's *dialogue.*

RICHARD: 'Madam, there is at the gate a young gentleman much desires to speak with you.'

KATHRYN: 'From the Count Orsino, is it?'

RICHARD: 'I know him not, Madam. Yon fellow swears he will speak with you. Lady, he's fortified against any denial.'

KATHRYN: 'Tell him he shall not speak with me!'

CAMERON: My fiancée has no wish to speak with you. What do you want?

RICHARD: 'He has been told so . . .'

CHARLOTTE: Little business between the lady an' me.

RICHARD: 'And he says he'll stand at your door like a sheriff's post, and be the supporter to a bench, but he'll speak with you.'

CAMERON: It's the end of the line for you, Badger!

CHARLOTTE: Is that so?

KATHRYN: 'What kind of man is he?'

RICHARD: 'Why, of mankind.'

CAMERON: I suggest you come with me!

> CAMERON *restrains* CHARLOTTE. *She struggles.*

KATHRYN: 'What manner of man?'

CHARLOTTE: Let go of me, prick!

> CHARLOTTE *breaks away, kneeing* CAMERON *in the process. She grabs* LUCY *and takes off.* CAMERON *yells.*

RICHARD: 'Of very ill manner.'

CAMERON: Bugger, bugger, bugger! Guard. Guard!

RICHARD: 'He'll speak with you, will you or no.'

KATHRYN: 'Of what personage and years is he?'

ADELAIDE *is half-dressed as Viola. She is about to put on Viola's jacket and a belt with a sheafed sword. During the following* CHARLOTTE *appears and grabs them from her. She runs to the stage, pulling the jacket on, and buckling up the belt and sword.*

RICHARD: 'Not yet old enough for a man, nor young enough for a boy. As a squash is to a peascod, or a codling when 'tis almost an apple; 'tis with him in standing water between boy and man. He is well-favoured and he speaks very shrewishly; one would think his mother's milk were scarce out of him.'

KATHRYN: 'Let him approach!'

RICHARD *starts to exit and* CHARLOTTE *comes hurtling into him.*

CHARLOTTE: Where is she?

RICHARD: I do beg your pardon?

CHARLOTTE: I wanna see her!

RICHARD: 'Of what . . . personage are you?'

CHARLOTTE: I *said*, I wanna see her!

RICHARD: 'The Honorable Lady of the house has no wish to see you, Sir! Leave here at once!'

CHARLOTTE: Listen fuck. Git outta my way.

KATHRYN: 'Who goes there, Malvolio?'

CHARLOTTE *pushes past him and boldly walks 'onstage'. She suddenly becomes aware of the audience and assumes a fake Shakespearean lingo.*

CHARLOTTE: 'Madame. Are you The Honorable Lady of the house?'

RICHARD *starts improvising.*

RICHARD: 'My lady. Shall I show him to door?'

KATHRYN *sees what's going on and intervenes.*

KATHRYN: 'Malvolio! I shall have an audience with Him! Her! Him!' (*To* CHARLOTTE.) 'Whence came you, Sir?' (*Under her breath.*) Are you mad? What are you doing here!

The real lines they say to each other are under their breath.

*The lines in inverted commas are performed in a theatrical
fashion.* RICHARD *rushes off.*

CHARLOTTE: I want the money. Where is it?

KATHRYN: 'I can say no more than I have studied, Sir, and that
question is out of my part.'

CHARLOTTE: You betrayed me, Lady!

KATHRYN: I tried to keep my word! It was not possible without
my fiancé finding out!

CHARLOTTE: You *lied* to me! *You* are a liar!

KATHRYN: 'No, my profound heart; and yet, Sir, by the very fangs
of malice I swear, that I am not that.' I kept my word. Now
get out of here before I go back on it and call the authorities.

CHARLOTTE: 'Thou art the devil!'

KATHRYN: 'Sir, I heard you were saucy at my gates! If you not be
mad, be gone. If you have reason, be brief.' You're ruining
my scene!

CHARLOTTE: I want wot I'm owed!

KATHRYN: Do you think I carry it on my person! ''Tis not that
time of moon with me, Sir, to make one in so skipping a
dialogue.'

KATHRYN *looks into the wings as she speaks.*

KATHRYN: The soldiers are looking for you. 'Will you hoist your
sail, Sir? Here lies a way.'

CHARLOTTE: I ain't leavin' till you give it.

KATHRYN: Do you want to be arrested!

CHARLOTTE *turns to go and sees the guards.*

CHARLOTTE: Christ Almighty! Place is crawling wi' soldiers!

CHARLOTTE *turns the other way, sees* CAPTAIN PETERS
looking for her and turns back again.

KATHRYN: 'Go good swabber! I pray you.'

CHARLOTTE: We had a bargain.

KATHRYN: 'Speak your office, Sir. What is your text?'

CHARLOTTE *looks wildly around her, sighting the guards in
every direction. She realises the only way to remain undetected
is to play the actor.*

CHARLOTTE: 'I see you what you are; you are too proud; but if you were the devil, you are fair.' Gawd it's that fiancé of yours. Don't let him see me.

> KATHRYN *picks up the dialogue with her in a very heightened fashion, amazed* CHARLOTTE *knows the lines.*

KATHRYN: 'Your Lord does know my mind; I cannot love him.' And I cannot produce money out of thin air!

CHARLOTTE: 'If I did love you in my master's flame, in your denial I would see no sense. I would . . . I would . . .'

> CHARLOTTE *looks round at* CAMERON *in the wings.*

KATHRYN: 'Why . . . What would you?'

> CHARLOTTE *goes down on one knee, and glancing back into the wings, picks up the scene.*

CHARLOTTE: 'Make me a willow cabin at your gate, And call upon my soul within the house; Write loyal cantons of condemned love and sing them loud even in the dead of night; Halloo your name to the reverberate hills. And make the babbling gossip of the air Cry out "Olivia!" O, you should not rest between the elements of air and earth, but you should pity me!'

> CHARLOTTE *realises she's about to be seen by* CAMERON. *She swings* KATHRYN *into a gallant and passionate kiss.* KATHRYN *is completely taken aback. She looks at* CHARLOTTE *in amazement, and like Olivia with Viola, she suddenly sees* CHARLOTTE *with new eyes.*
>
> *Pause.*

KATHRYN: 'Oh . . . You might do much . . .'

> *Pause.* KATHRYN *stumbles through her next lines.*

KATHRYN: 'Get you to your Lord. I cannot love him; let him send no more.' Meet me at the gate. 'Unless perchance you come to me again to tell me how he takes it.' I'll get it for you. 'Fare you well.'

> CAMERON *comes rushing on and sees* CHARLOTTE. *He realises he's onstage and starts spouting Shakespearean vitriol.*

CAMERON: 'Ah! There you are you blackguard!'

CHARLOTTE: Not you again, prick.

CAMERON: 'Thou thought thou hast escaped, didst thou? Come, Sir, I would not be in your coat for tuppence! If thou dar'st tempt me further, draw thy sword. Come, Sir, put up your iron. You are well fleshed!'

They circle one another. CAMERON *reaches for the sword on his belt and unsheathes it.* CHARLOTTE *circles him and draws her sword. They circle, fight,* CAMERON *quoting Shakespeare.*

CAMERON: 'Ungracious fiend! Fit for the mountains and the barbarous caves, where manners ne'er were preached!'

KATHRYN: 'Hold thee! I charge thee! On my life I charge thee! Hold!'

It is a great sword fight, the two being adept with a sword, CAMERON *because of his stage training and* CHARLOTTE *because of her experiences.* CHARLOTTE *sees* LUCY *and is mindful of protecting her, she speaks to her and continues to fight.*

CHARLOTTE: Haere atu, Lucy! E haere! (Go away from here, Lucy! Go away!) Koe! (You!)

CAMERON *gets the better of* CHARLOTTE *as she's talking to* LUCY.

CAMERON: 'Out of my sight! You unnatural wench!'

CHARLOTTE *drops her sword and doubles in pain.*

KATHRYN: Cameron!

CAPTAIN PETERS *comes on and addresses the audience.*

CAPTAIN PETERS: Gentlemen, we must stop the performance! One of our men has been killed on Wairoa Road. A Maori raiding party is due to attack Williamson's clearing. All men are to report to duty.

LUCY *runs to* CHARLOTTE.

CHARLOTTE: E oma, Lucy. (Run, Lucy.) E oma. (Run.)

CAMERON: Captain, this woman's in cahoots with the natives.

CHARLOTTE: Kia tere, Lucy. Kia tere. (Quick, Lucy.)

LUCY *is grabbed by a guard.*

CAPTAIN PETERS: Guards! Guards!

CHARLOTTE, *screams out:* Leave 'er! Leave 'er alone!

> *There is a lighting change. Stark, threatening. Two* MASKED
> CORPORALS *appear, pointing guns at* CHARLOTTE. *They
> move in rhythmic steps, closing in. They move in and beat
> her to the floor in a stylistic fashion.* KATHRYN *grabs* LUCY
> *and shields her eyes from the beating. Drums, chants, war
> cries. A Union Jack is either brought on or dropped from the
> ceiling.* CAPTAIN PETERS, CAMERON *and the* MASKED
> CORPORALS *stand staunchly, facing out front. They sing 'Rule
> Britannia' in fervent patriotic tones. The song builds, swelling
> to a climax.* KATHRYN *doesn't sing.*

Scene 17: Albert Barracks—Auckland

KATHRYN *is standing alone, her arms wrapped around herself.*
CAPTAIN PETERS, CAMERON *and* LUCY *enter.* CAPTAIN PETERS *has
a restraining hand on* LUCY'S *neck.*

CAPTAIN PETERS, *entering:* We've locked her in one of the
    storehouses until she can be conveyed handcuffed to the
    police office.

KATHRYN: But the child. What will become of the child?

CAPTAIN PETERS: She'll be taken to the local missionaries.

CAMERON: She'll be a damn sight better off.

KATHRYN: You can't take her from her mother, surely.

CAMERON: Captain, in the light of this recent incident, we shall
    be cutting this tour short. We'll set sail for San Francisco
    tomorrow.

> KATHRYN *looks alarmed.*

KATHRYN: Tomorrow?

CAPTAIN PETERS: There's a brig sailing in the morning.

KATHRYN: The morning? I can't leave in the morning. I don't have
    my . . . *(She is about to say: my papers.)*

CAMERON: What don't you have?

KATHRYN: Nothing. It's just . . . it's just a little soon that's all. We're due to perform with Mr George Buckingham! We can't let him down, surely!

CAMERON: Unforeseen circumstances. Buckingham will understand.

KATHRYN: Cammy, we can't! I have things to attend to . . .

CAMERON: What things?

> KATHRYN *can't bring herself to say that she's given her papers to Charlotte.*

CAMERON: I'll go and pack the trunks.

> *He starts to go.*

KATHRYN: Cameron! We cannot possible leave with such haste.

CAMERON: It's not prudent to stay in a town on the brink of war!

KATHRYN: There are other members of this company to take into account!

CAMERON: I'll talk to Adelaide, of course!

KATHRYN: Talk to her then! Go on! Don't mind what I think! Why should you? You never do! My opinion doesn't count, does it!

CAMERON: Kathryn.

KATHRYN: Does it?

CAMERON: Kathryn, I am packing the trunks and I suggest you get out of your costume and pack your make-up.

> CAMERON *leaves.* CAPTAIN PETERS, *who is still standing there a little embarrassed, clears his throat.*

CAPTAIN PETERS: Mr Carruthers is right, Miss. It's not a safe place under the circumstances.

> KATHRYN *looks desperately at* CAPTAIN PETERS.

KATHRYN: Captain, is there any way I can visit the prisoner? Just for a moment please. It really is urgent.

CAPTAIN PETERS: I'm afraid not, Miss.

KATHRYN: Captain, please. I can't explain. I can't possibly leave unless I see her.

CAPTAIN PETERS: Well . . . I suppose it can't do any harm. There's a guard on duty, so you'll be quite safe. I'll have to take you over there myself.

KATHRYN: Thank you, Captain. Thank you.

CAPTAIN PETERS: And you will have to accompany me, Missy, until I find someone to take you over to the local Mission House.

> CAPTAIN PETERS, KATHRYN *and* LUCY *exit.*

Scene 18: Blockhouse—Albert Barracks

CHARLOTTE *is lying on the ground in the dark when* KATHRYN *comes in. Her ankles and hands are tied. She turns away from* KATHRYN *as she comes in.* KATHRYN *can hardly see at first.*

KATHRYN: I've come for my papers.

CHARLOTTE: I din't think this was a social visit.

KATHRYN: You won't be needing them for the sailing ship now.

CHARLOTTE: Don't expect I shall. I'm becalmed in't I? I run aground, thanks to you.

KATHRYN: I didn't betray you

CHARLOTTE: Take the papers. They're in me pocket.

KATHRYN: You must believe me.

CHARLOTTE: I'd hand them over nicely, only I'm a bit trussed up at the moment.

KATHRYN: I had the money all ready to give to you, when my fiancé came looking for me. What was I to do?

> KATHRYN *has come close enough to see her and is appalled.*

CHARLOTTE: Just take 'em!

> KATHRYN *leans down to get them out of her pocket.*

KATHRYN: Oh God. What have they done to you?

> KATHRYN *goes over to her and unties her wrists and ankles.*

KATHRYN: My God, you're a mess. These are so tight, they're restricting your circulation.

> KATHRYN *gets the ropes off and speaks in an authoritative voice.*

KATHRYN: Sit up!

CHARLOTTE: Wot?
KATHRYN: I said, sit up! You're bleeding.

CHARLOTTE *sits up and* KATHRYN *gets out a handkerchief.*

CHARLOTTE: Can't feel a thing.

KATHRYN *dabs at the wound above* CHARLOTTE'*s eye.*

CHARLOTTE: Ow!
KATHRYN: Keep still.

KATHRYN *continues to dab in silence at the wound.*

KATHRYN: There. That's stopping it a bit.

CHARLOTTE *sits still as* KATHRYN *works. Silence.*

CHARLOTTE: Never had no one tend me before.
KATHRYN: Well don't get any funny ideas.
CHARLOTTE, *smiles:* Wot funny ideas would I get?
KATHRYN: You know perfectly well what I mean!
CHARLOTTE: Can't for the life of me imagine.

KATHRYN *continues to dab in silence.*

CHARLOTTE: You don't 'alf have soft hands.
KATHRYN: No, I don't half!

CHARLOTTE *takes* KATHRYN'*s hand and kisses it.* KATHRYN
is taken aback, but doesn't stop her. She swallows.

KATHRYN: That's because I . . . because I play the pianoforte . . .
one must take good care of one's hands . . . if one plays the
pianoforte one's hands must be soft, light, dexterous . . .
dexterous, in order to be truly articulate . . .

CHARLOTTE *keeps kissing* KATHRYN'*s fingers as she speaks.*

KATHRYN: . . . one must be able to . . . to speak with one's fingers
you see . . . to caress Beethoven, stroke Bach . . . to feel
with the lightest, lightest touch, in order to lift the music
into life . . .

KATHRYN'*s voice goes up a few decibels as* CHARLOTTE *undoes
the top of her blouse and kisses her neck.*

KATHRYN: . . . One must . . . feel it in one's whole body . . . not just one's fingers, it's a physical sensation you see . . . a physical sensation that . . . that extends . . . extends to the extreme extremities . . . oh dear, oh dear . . .

GUARD, *voice off*: Are you ready to come out, Miss?

KATHRYN calls to him.

KATHRYN: No! Not quite! Just a few more moments!

Pause. KATHRYN pulls herself together. CHARLOTTE takes the papers and hands them to KATHRYN.

CHARLOTTE: Here's the papers to freedom.

KATHRYN: Thank you!

Pause.

CHARLOTTE: What you waitin' for?

KATHRYN: Nothing.

CHARLOTTE: Off you go then.

KATHRYN: I'm going.

CHARLOTTE: Go then.

KATHRYN: That's good.

Pause.

KATHRYN: Well, good luck then.

CHARLOTTE: Ta. You too.

KATHRYN: And I hope . . . I hope I never have to see you again!

CHARLOTTE: I hope so too.

KATHRYN: I shall be pleased to see the back of you.

CHARLOTTE: You don't look pleased.

KATHRYN: It is in my nature to be either very happy or very miserable. And at the moment I am very miserable, on account of being very tired!

CHARLOTTE: Pleasant dreams then!

KATHRYN: Thank you!

CHARLOTTE, *she calls after her*: Oh, an' I hope you an' the Gov' have a very nice life together.

KATHRYN: I expect we shall!

CHARLOTTE: Though I ain't never seen two people less suited. You is as like as an oyster is to an apple.

KATHRYN: Is that so?
CHARLOTTE: Yeah, but you get that.
KATHRYN: You do, yes . . .
CHARLOTTE: Yes.

> *Pause.* KATHRYN *hesitates.*

KATHRYN: Do you think that . . . do you think that people who
are so awfully ill-suited could . . . could possibly have anything
in common?
CHARLOTTE: Not usual, no.
KATHRYN: No. Neither do I.

> *Pause.*

CHARLOTTE: But then they do say that opposites attract, don't
they?
KATHRYN: Yes. Yes, they do.
CHARLOTTE: But I don't believe that. Do you?
KATHRYN: No.
CHARLOTTE: Right then. You got the papers then.

> KATHRYN *hesitates. She realises that she does not want to go
> back to London.*

KATHRYN: Take them. They're yours really.
CHARLOTTE: Wot?
KATHRYN: I want you to keep them.
CHARLOTTE: Can't use them where I'm going.

> KATHRYN *looks back towards the door, knowing she can help*
> CHARLOTTE *escape. Pause.* KATHRYN*'s mind is ticking over
> furiously.*

KATHRYN: Charlotte. When you came onstage tonight . . . when
you enacted that scene with me . . . you had something of
the actor in you, didn't you?
CHARLOTTE: It's in me blood, acting! It's a bit like lyin' in't it?
KATHRYN: A little bit, yes.
CHARLOTTE: Done it all me life then.
KATHRYN: Yes, you do have a natural ability to dramatise!

> KATHRYN *laughs.*

CHARLOTTE: When you laugh, you remind me of a scrubber I once knew.
KATHRYN: You, thank God, don't remind me of anyone!
CHARLOTTE: You never been down Devils Acre then! Get plenty like me down there.
KATHRYN: I doubt it somehow.
CHARLOTTE: You really are pretty when you smile.

> KATHRYN *smiles again, but this time rather shyly.*

KATHRYN: Am I?

> CHARLOTTE *caresses* KATHRYN*'s cheek as the lights fade and the drums beat.*

Scene 19: Dressing Room

RICHARD *is standing looking expectant.* ADELAIDE *runs her fingers through his hair.*

RICHARD: Adelaide, what can possibly be so hard to say?
ADELAIDE: Richard. Cameron believes we should cancel the rest of the tour. He wants to move on to San Francisco as soon as possible.
RICHARD: Oh.

> *Pause.*

ADELAIDE: There's a boat leaving in the morning . . .
RICHARD: Oh I see . . .

> *Silence between them.*

ADELAIDE: Say something Richard, please.
RICHARD: What should I say? I always knew I had borrowed time, but I didn't know it was quite this borrowed . . . I thought we might have had a little longer . . . another month perhaps . . . maybe more . . .
ADELAIDE: Richard. You are a sensitive and beautiful man.

> *Pause.*

RICHARD: But that's not what you want is it?

ADELAIDE: Of course it is.

RICHARD: Then why not stay here? Why go back? Why not stay
here with me? We could . . .

ADELAIDE: Richard. Richard, you live here. You are happy here. I
would die without my London . . .

RICHARD: Then I could come to London! Sell up the business . . .
I could . . .

ADELAIDE: It wouldn't work, Richard. You know it wouldn't.

Pause. RICHARD *looks away as he speaks.*

RICHARD: I had hoped . . . I had hoped I might be the man you
spoke of. The one you'd always wanted to know . . . Foolish
dreamer, me. I might've known I suppose. A woman like
you. What would you see in . . .

ADELAIDE: I shall always think of you with a great deal of affection.

RICHARD *scoffs.*

RICHARD: Affection!

ADELAIDE: Richard, please . . .

RICHARD: It's someone like Carruthers you want, isn't it?

ADELAIDE: Don't be absurd.

RICHARD: Someone who treats you badly. It's him that you want,
isn't it?

ADELAIDE: If I wanted Cameron, Richard, I would still have him.

Pause.

RICHARD: Oh. Oh, I see. What a fool I am.

ADELAIDE: I have loved our time together. Please don't spoil it.

Pause. RICHARD *looks away.*

ADELAIDE: Please don't make it hard for me . . .

Pause.

ADELAIDE: Say something. Please!

RICHARD *looks at her with a sad smile.*

RICHARD: 'Before our lives divide forever. I will say no more
than a man might say, whose whole life's love goes down in
a day . . .'

ADELAIDE: Richard . . .

RICHARD: Like the actor on the stage, when we are done we are forgotten . . .

ADELAIDE: Don't . . .

RICHARD: We leave no trace of our brief and happy reign behind us . . .

> *She touches his face tenderly. He turns his face away then leaves.* ADELAIDE *is left alone, visibly upset.*

Scene 20: Blockhouse—Albert Barracks

CAMERON's *voice is heard in the darkness.*

CAMERON, *off*: Let me in you bloody idiot! I refuse to let you keep her here!

> *When the lights come up,* KATHRYN *is sitting, wearing* CHARLOTTE's *clothes with the Shakespearean jacket, staring into the middle distance, pensive.* CAMERON *comes rushing in.*

RICHARD: Lunatic! Absolute lunatic! That idiot guard has been trying to convince me you aided and abetted a criminal! He says she could never have gotten out of the ropes unless you'd helped her. Nearly punched his nose! Damned clown claims you helped her escape!

> *Pause.*

KATHRYN: I did.

CAMERON: What?

KATHRYN: I did help her.

> *Pause.* CAMERON *takes a moment for this to sink in. He talks quietly.*

CAMERON: Oh God, Kathryn.

> *Pause.* CAMERON *continues to speak quietly and deliberately.*

CAMERON: I have just spent twenty minutes convincing that lame lieutenant that my fiancée is an honest woman! He was ready to cart you off to the local lock-up! How could you sink to such unfathomable depths of depravity?

KATHRYN: If that woman had anything like the chances you and I have had . . .

CAMERON: It wouldn't make the blindest bit of difference! Come on! I'm getting you out of here!

KATHRYN: But I am to be locked up, surely?

CAMERON: Oh don't be absurd, Kathryn! I've paid the blighter thirty guineas!

KATHRYN: God, God, Cameron! Can't you *see?*

CAMERON: I see that you're overwrought. I see that we need to get out of this horrid little lock-up. And I see that we need to quit this convoluted colony as soon as humanly possible!

KATHRYN: How is it that *I* can buy my way out of here? But *she* cannot! Don't you *understand,* Cammy?

CAMERON: I understand that you've picked up some ridiculous romantic notion about the lower classes! It's in her blood, darling. You've been corrupted by a very clever criminal. By the whole colony in fact! It's a horrid little hotchpotch of a place all mixed up together.

KATHRYN: But that's what I like about it! The fact that it *is* mixed up!

CAMERON: It's all upside down. It wouldn't surprise me if one day it was run by women!

Pause.

KATHRYN: I want to stay here, Cammy.

CAMERON: Kathryn, we can't possibly stay. It has none of the comforts of England. We'd miss the theatre, the society, the culture. I simply could not abide it.

Pause.

KATHRYN: No. But I could.

CAMERON: Don't be absurd!

KATHRYN: I could teach singing and music. I've thought about it, Cameron. While I was sitting here in the dark.

She looks at him sadly.

CAMERON: But . . . but what about us?

KATHRYN: Oh, darling. I'm not what you want . . .

CAMERON: That's not true, Kathryn . . .

KATHRYN: If you are honest with yourself you'll know who you really want. Oh, darling, it's not that we've stopped loving each other, we will never do that, but that we've stopped *seeing* one another. We have come to see only what we want to see, Cammy.

> CAMERON *is staggered.*

CAMERON: That happens, Kathryn . . . over time . . . it's normal.

KATHRYN: I want more, darling. I want to be made love to and desired, not just adored like a prized possession. I want us to *grow* together, not drift into marriage because it's inevitable. And then find that we must stay together because we once said we would . . . too scared to ever leave. You would only want other women eventually. And I would only feel trapped . . .

CAMERON: But . . . but, you can't stay here alone . . .

> *Pause.*

KATHRYN: I am done with England, darling.

> *Pause.* CAMERON *sees she is serious. He doesn't know what to say.*

CAMERON: I . . . I can't accept this . . . I can't . . .

> *He looks grief stricken.* KATHRYN *looks at him in compassion and in her own grief. Pause.*

CAMERON: I have expected too much of you. I can see that. I can stop the drinking. You know I can. It will be alright. But let's get out of this hateful little lock-up before the guard changes his mind.

KATHRYN: Oh, Cammy.

> *She puts her arms around him.*

CAMERON: Come on darling, come on, we'll talk I promise.

> *He starts to lead* KATHRYN *out by the arm, then sees something lying on the ground.*

CAMERON: It's this place, I swear.

> CAMERON *bends down to pick something up.*

CAMERON: Here. What's this? It's your papers. You've dropped your papers, darling. Come on.

> KATHRYN *looks at them appalled.*

KATHRYN: Oh my God! Look I'll . . . I'll meet you back in the dressing room!

> *She runs out.* CAMERON *calls after her.*

CAMERON: Kathryn! Where are you going? Kathryn!

Scene 21: Wharf—Auckland

CHARLOTTE *enters the wharf area dressed in* KATHRYN'*s clothes.* LUCY *is beside her, wrapped in a blanket.* KATHRYN *runs on.* CHARLOTTE *looks amused when she sees her.*

KATHRYN: You forgot this . . .
CHARLOTTE: If I din't know better, I'd think you was following us!
KATHRYN: You wouldn't get far without them.

> CHARLOTTE *takes them.*

CHARLOTTE: Why 'ave you helped us?
KATHRYN: Because . . . Because . . . Well I can't say exactly . . . Because I think your penalty is too harsh for your deeds.
CHARLOTTE: Like you said, I ain't no saint.
KATHRYN: Nevertheless, if you were allowed to live with dignity, you might at least have the opportunity to live an honest life.

> CHARLOTTE *grins.*

CHARLOTTE: Not sure I want an honest life.
KATHRYN: I think you do.
CHARLOTTE: It's not honest, me travelling on your papers is it? Not honest a' you neither.

> KATHRYN *laughs.*

KATHRYN: That's different! Let's not speak about that.
CHARLOTTE: Why's that different?
KATHRYN: Just accept it and stop asking silly questions.
CHARLOTTE: Right then.
KATHRYN: Right.

> *They stand awkwardly, not knowing what to say next.*

CHARLOTTE: So. So you staying here then.
KATHRYN: Yes. Yes, I have decided.
CHARLOTTE: Quickest decision I ever saw.
KATHRYN: I think I made it a long time ago, only I didn't care to
see it . . .

> *Pause.* KATHRYN *hands her the Shakespearean book.*

KATHRYN: I brought you the book . . .
CHARLOTTE: Can't read, can I.

> *Pause.* KATHRYN *looks awkward for a moment then hands
the book to her.*

KATHRYN: I'd like you to have it . . .

> *Awkward pause.*

KATHRYN: It contains that speech you memorised so well, 'Make
me a willow cabin at your gate . . .'

> CHARLOTTE *takes the book and picks up the line before*
> KATHRYN *has a chance to finish it.*

CHARLOTTE: 'And call upon your soul within the house . . .'
KATHRYN: 'My' soul.
CHARLOTTE: Wot?
KATHRYN: It's 'my' soul, not 'your' soul.
CHARLOTTE: Yeah, yeah I know that, but that don't make sense
see. Cause it's you wot's in the house, while I'm there in the
cabin, so I puts 'your' soul in there instead, see. Cause it's
your soul I'm calling. Cause that makes sense see?

> KATHRYN*'s laugh has a tender tone.*

KATHRYN: Yes, yes I do see. You're right. 'Your' soul is much better.
I don't know why Mr Shakespeare didn't . . . why he didn't

put that there in the first place . . . Poets! Really. What on earth was the man thinking of . . .?

> KATHRYN *trails out. There is a pause.* CHARLOTTE *looks at the book.*

CHARLOTTE: Well, then . . . You never know, it might come in handy . . . light a fire with it . . . trade it in for something useful . . .

KATHRYN: Yes, all that . . . *(Pause.)* And this is for you.

> KATHRYN *holds out the locket.*

CHARLOTTE: She'll just lose that.

KATHRYN: Doesn't matter. Go on, Lucy. Take it.

> *She hands* LUCY *the locket.*

CHARLOTTE: Ta.

> *Pause.*

KATHRYN: You'll be a passenger this time.

CHARLOTTE: Aye.

> *Pause.*

KATHRYN: Well then . . .

CHARLOTTE: Well . . .

> *Silence. The two women stand looking at each other. Each in Shakespearean costume. Two women who, for that solitary moment, have bridged an unspoken divide.*

KATHRYN: Goodbye, Charlotte.

CHARLOTTE: Goodbye, Kathryn.

> *They stand still looking at each other as* ADELAIDE*'s operatic aria floats in and the lights fade.*